THE HISTORY OF COVENTRY [BY B. POOLE].

Publisher's Note

The book descriptions we ask book-sellers to display prominently warn that this is an historic book with numerous typos or missing text; it is not indexed or illustrated.

The book was created using optical character recognition software. The software is 99 percent accurate if the book is in good condition. However, we do understand that even one percent can be an annoying number of typos! And sometimes all or part of a page may be missing from our copy of the book. Or the paper may be so discolored from age that it is difficult to read. We apologize and gratefully acknowledge Google's assistance.

After we re-typeset and design a book, the page numbers change so the old index and table of contents no longer work. Therefore, we often remove them; otherwise, please ignore them.

Our books sell so few copies that you would have to pay hundreds of dollars to cover the cost of our proof reading and fixing the typos, missing text and index. Instead we let most customers download a free copy of the original typo-free scanned book. Simply enter the barcode number from the back cover of the paperback in the Free Book form at www.RareBooksClub.com. You may also qualify for a free trial membership in our book club to download up to four books for free. Simply enter the barcode number from the back cover onto the membership form on our home page. The book club entitles you to select from more than a million books at no additional charge. Simply enter the title or subject onto the search form to find the books.

If you have any questions, could you please be so kind as to consult our Frequently Asked Questions page at www. RareBooksClub.com/faqs.cfm? You are also welcome to contact us there.

General Books LLC™, Memphis, USA, 2012.

☙ ☙ ☙ ☙ ☙ ☙ ☙ ☙

HISTORY OF COVENTRY, BEING A CONCISE ACCOUNT Or THE Snrirat StoriMmu, Customs, nbliE 3Jniliings, OF THE CITY, AND A COMPLETE EPITOME OF MODERN CHANGES; TOGETHER WITH AN APPENDIX, INCLUDING A COPIOUS AND INTERESTING CHRONOLOGY OF LOCAL OCCURRENCES.

COVENTRY: PRINTED AND PUBLISHED BY D. LEWIN, HERTFORD STREET. AUTHOR'S PREFACE.

The present publication being accompanied by an *Appendix,* requires a few prefatory remarks. The first issue of 1847, in bound-up volumes entire, being sold off, the Proprietor determined to send out the remaining portion of the edition in numbers, with a view of rendering its circulation more convenient to the working classes of his fellow-townsmen; for perhaps there is no topic upon which even the *reading* public of Coventry are so much in the dark, as that of the History of their own City; and yet there is none with which they ought to be more conversant. In making this second issue in numbers, it was at the same time determined to add a supplementary Appendix, furnishing such corrective or explanatory remarks to the first publication as had become necessary, and comprising all the *additional matters of History* in connexion with the town, which has occurred since the month of July, 1847,—an interval replete with incidents and changes, of great interest, and equal importance.

In perusing the *Appendix* therefore, it must be borne in mind, that its compilation took plaoe from four to five years after the first part of the work; which will account for some passages and statements appearing as it were disconnected from the relative portion of the same subject in the antecedent pages. Should a reprint of the work be called for, this defect will be obviated by a re-arrangement of the entire contents.

The main object of the Appendix is, to place upon record the facts worthy of notice: which it is hoped will prove of some advantage to the local public. By the turning over of a few pages, backwards or forwards, the reader will be enabled without much difficulty, to connect the particular subjects, (as those of the principal parish churches for instance,) which, under the circumstances described, are divided. It should also be understood, that nearly twelve months elapsed between the printing of the first and the last sheets of the Appendix.

BENJN. POOLE.

October, 1852.

CONTENTS.

Page in

Page. Appendix.

Engraving— View of Coventry J

Preface 2

Introduction..... 3

Antiquity of Coventry... 4

Position and General Appeara.icc--6

Ancient Convent and Cathedral 7 12

Lady Godiva and Peeping Tom *(with engraving)* 9

Woodcut of Peeping Tom ---11

Order of the Godiva Procession *(with engraving)* -----14

Manor of Cheylesmore and Park-17

Great Fair 21

City Walls and Gates *(with four woodcuts)* 22

Incorporation by Edward 1H--29

Charter of Henry VI----ib.

Boundaries of Coventry, past and present 31

Monastic Institutions—

The Priory.... 36

Woodcut of Cathedral Remains. 41
Grey Friars.... ib.
White Friars' Monastery *(withwoodcut)* 43
Woodcut of Old Gateway --44
Carthusian Monastery, orCharter House 45
The Cross *(with woodcut)* 47
Spon Hospital-----49
Ford's Hospital *(with woodcut and engraving)* .... 5(1
Bond's Hospital *(with woodcut)* 52
St. John's Hospital—the Free School *(with woodcut)* 54
The Gilds—St. Mary's Hail *(with woodcut and engraving)* ----58
Page in
Page. Appendix.
Drapers' Hall-----
County Hall *(with woodcut)*-
The Gaol-----
St. Michael's Church *(with engraving)* -
Trinity Church *(with engraving)*
Trinity Church Schools-
St. John's Church *(with engraving)*-
Christ Church *(with engraving)*-
St. Peter's Church-
District of St. Thomas----
Dissenting Places of Worship—
The Great Meeting-
Vicar-lane Chapel-
West-orchard Chapel
The Friends' Meeting House-
Cow-lane Cbapel-
Wesley Chapel-
Spon-end Chapel
White Friars'-lane Chapel
Well-street Chapel-
Grove-street Chapel-
Hill-field Chapel---
Roman Catholic Church *(with engraving)*-
Endowed Schools—
Bablake School-
Baker, Billing, and Crow's
Blue Coat Girls
Bayley's Charity-
Southern and Craner's
Fairfax's Charity-
, Unendowed Schools—
British School----

The National Schools
St. John's Day and Sunday Schools
Roman Catholic Schools-
Infant Schools----
School of Design-
Mechanics' Institution-
Religious and Useful Knowledge Society-
Coventry Subscription Library
The Barracks *(with woodcut)*
Page in
Page. Appendix.
Post Office 100
Theatre 103
Gas Works..... jo.
Waterworks..... 105
Cemetery *(with engraving)* 106 8
Baths *faith engraving J* ... 27
Railway Station----110
The Canal Ill
Banks 112
Savings' Bank-----113
Medical Institutions—
Provident Dispensary--ib.
Coventry and Warwickshire Hospital 115
Lying-in Charities---110
Industrial Home----ib.
Provident Institution and Loan Society 117
The Coventry Charities--118
Trustees of Sir T. White's Estates-120
Trustees of Church Charities-121
Trustees of General Charities--ib.
Lammas Lands....-122
Seniority Fund.... 123
Magistracy-----124
Corporation-----125
Directors of the Poor----126
Trades of Coventry-ib.
Bishopric of Coventry... 130
Earldom of Coventry... 131
Fairs, Races, &c.----132
Inns—Newspapers-133
Population—Distance from London—Market Days 135 25
Parliamentary Representatives--136 26—30
Chronology of Events----148 13
Eminent Natives of Coventry--169
City Arms *(with woodcut and engraving)* 170
City Revenue-----ib.

THE HISTORY OF COVENTRY.

IN presenting to the public a concise *History of*

I *the City of Coventry,* embracing an epitome of its ancient history and greatness, and supplying a directory to the interesting relics of antiquity which it still affords, as well as to its existing institutions, the compiler of the present work will *invent* nothing by way of an affectation of originality as to matters of fact; but, nevertheless, being aware that there are extensive stores of information which are as yet but little known, his object will be to draw therefrom, and to arrange the contents of these pages with such clearness, that all the main points of the subject shall make a fixed impression on the mind of the reader, and be easy for reference. At the same time, a considerable amount of *new* intelligence i—intelligence which has never before appeared in any work of this kind,—will be supplied here in many of the sections, according to the order in which they are given.

This task cannot be more appropriately commenced, than by quoting the initiatory passage from the great work of our eminent local historian Sir William Dugdale, who, writing nearly two hundred years ago, in his own quaint terms and form of expression, observes, on the ANTIQUITY OF COVENTRY:

"Coventre is still a City of eminent note, yet much short in glory and riches to what heretofore it hath been, as I shall show anon: but for the originall of its name I can give no positive reason; and therefore, whither the first part thereof, viz., Coven, was occasioned by some Covent of religious persons, antiently founded here, as some think; for there was a Monastery of Nuns long before the Priory, as I shall shortly manifest; or whither from this little brook *Shirburn,* of which others conceive the true name to be Ccne, I will not stand to argue. Sure I am, that the last sillable thereof, *viz., Tre,* is British, and signifieth the same that *Villa* in Latine doth: from whence I conclude that the first plantation here, hath been of very great antiquity, though when, or by whom made I cannot expect to discover, having so little light of story to guide me through these elder times. And as certain is it that a great part thereof, and probably the most antient, stood on the bank without Bishop-gate, northwestward of the City; for no less do the foundations of much building there discovered, and a place yet called St. Nicholas Church-yard, testify."

As further investigation into the origin of the *name* of Coventry is not very important, and would probably yield nothing more satisfactory, the above passage on this point may sufiice. According to Camden, however, the name in early history was written *Conventria;* and with respect to "the most ancient" part here alluded to, the traces of extensive foundations at the north-west extremity of the City which still remain,— (the spot on which Trinity Vicarage-house now stands,)—sufficiently indicate that the supposition as to a large portion of its former site being in that direction, is well founded.

ITS POSITION AND GENERAL APPEARAN
Coventry is for the most part elig situated on a gentle eminence, rising in 1 centre of a valley, stretching from east to wt and bounded to the north-west by the rr Sherbourne and the Radford brook, whi unite within the town; and passing throu it in an easterly direction, the stream fa into the river Avon at Stoneleigh, about fo miles distant from the City. Its greate length is from Spon-end to Far Gosford-stree or Gosford-green, measuring almost two mile in length, and its principal intersection is fron north to south, about three quarters of a mile. It is nearly in the centre of England, on a tract about three hundred feet above the sea level; the surface of the surrounding country being a gentle hill and dale, with a rich undulating and pleasing appearance, which is greatly heightened by numerous small spots of woodland. The town is very irregularly built, many of the older houses being constructed in the style of the 15th and 16th centuries, formed with a ponderous timber framework, filled up with brick and plaster, and the upper stories projecting over each other into the streets; giving to them, in most cases, a dark and gloomy character, though in some instances

these curious specimens of the antique fashion of building are not destitute of interest to the passing visitor.

Amongst the many proofs on record of the important position once occupied by this City, it is worth remark, that by the roll-tax of 1377, in the notices which it contains of the population of all the principal towns, Coventry appears third on the list in point of magnitude, next to London; York and Bristol being the only two taking precedence of it. That the eminence to which Coventry in former times had attained, was mainly attributable to its religious establishments, is abundantly manifest.

ANCIENT CONVENT.
Even as early as the ninth century of the christian era it is certain that an important Convent of Nuns existed here, and which, as Leland states, was founded by King Canute. Touching this house of nuns, Dugdale says, "I find that in the year of Christ 1016 that infamous traytor, Edricus, invaded Mercia with an army, burnt and wasted various towns in Warvvickshire, at which time the said house of nun whereof St. Osburg, a holy virgin, had bee sometime abbess, was destroyed."

It was on the ruins of this convent tha Leofric, the fifth Earl of Mercia, conjointly witJ his Countess Godiva, in the year 1044, and it the reign of Edward the Confessor, founded, and richly endowed the monastery for Benedictine Monks; which, for the greatness of its revenues, and the splendour of its ornaments, was scarcely surpassed by any in the kingdom. On the nature of its embellishments, William of Malmsbury observes, that "it was enriched and beautified with so much gold and silver, that the walls seemed too narrow to contain it: insomuch that Robert de Limesi, (a mercenary bishop of the diocese in the time of King William Rufus,) scraped from one beam that supported the shrines, 500 marks of silver." Amongst the reliqaes, and placed on a silver.shrine, was an arm of St. Augustine, with an inscription, purporting "that it was purchased by Agelnethus, Archbishop of Canterbury, in 1020, from the Pope at Rome, for the sum of.

one talent of silver and two hundred talents of gold."

But besides the religious benefactions of

Leofric and Godiva, there is a more notable act ascribed to the noble lady, which Dugdale thus relates:— LADY GODIVA AND PEEPING TOM.

"The Countess Godiva, bearing an extraordinary affection for this place (Coventry), often and earnestly besought her husband, that for the love of God and the blessed Virgin, he would free it from that grievous servitude whereunto it was subject; but he, rebuking her for importuning him in a matter inconsistent with his profit, commanded that she should henceforth forbear to move therein; yet she, out of her womanish pertinacity, continued to solicit him, insomuch that he told her, if she would consent to ride naked from one end of the town to the other, in the sight of all the people, he would grant her request. Whereupon she returned, *'But mill you give me leave so to do V* and he replying *yes,* the noble lady, upon an appointed day, got on horseback naked, with her hair loose, so that it covered all her body but the legs, and thus performing her journey, returned with joy to her husband: who thereupon granted to the inhabitants a Charter of Freedom, which immunity I rather conceive to have been a kiud of manumission from some servile tenure, whereby they then held what they had under this great Earl, than onely a freedom from all manner of toll, except horses, as *Knighton* affirms: in memory whereof the picture of him and his said Lady were set up in a south window of Trinity Church, in this City, about Richard II.'s time, and his right hand holding a Charter with these words written thereon:— J ittmcfje *fov* Uobe of *fQte* ZEtoe matte tfobentre foWm."

Only some faint traces of these portraits and inscription now remain in the window of Trinity Church here pointed out.

Time, and the love of fiction, have made a considerable addition to this account of the singular feat of Godiva in behalf of her favourite City; for upon it has been engrafted the story of " Peeping Tom," setting forth that, previous to Godiva's riding through the town, all persons were commanded to keep within doors, and from their windows, during her progress; but that a certain tailor, who must needs be peeping, looked out, upon which the lady's horse neighed, and the tailor paid for his curiosity and presumption by the loss of his sight. In conformity with this traditionary tale, a figure called "Peeping Tom" is placed at an opening in the upper part of a house now forming the corner of Hertford-street; and the remembrance of Godiva's regard is preserved by the occasional exhibition, during the Great Fair, of a long and showy procession, in the midst of which a female, representing the Countess, rides through the streets, adorned with long and flowing hair, and habited in a linen or silk dress, closely fitted to the body. This public exhibition of Lady Godiva in a procession, was first instituted in the reign of the licentious monarch Charles the Second. It will be found now transformed into a cocked hat and wig) on his head, greaves on his legs, and sandals on his feet; but to favour the posture of leaning out of a window, the arms have been cut off at the elbows. From the attitude in which it was originally carved, there is reason to believe that it was either intended for Mars, the fabulous god of war, or some other warlike chieftain. Certain it is, that such a figure was never exhibited in this habit and situation to resemble a mechanic.

The love of gorgeous shows, for which Coventry has always been celebrated, is inseperably connected with its history, as particularly attested in the records respecting its ancient mysteries or religious dramas, which were performed on moveable stages, and consequently exhibited in various parts of the City. In these performances, which were got up chiefly by the Grey Friars on the day of Corpus Christi, were represented the nativity, crucifixion, the resurrection, day of judgment, and such like subjects, all acted out with such gravity and grandeur as to become worthy the attention of kings, queens, and nobles, who frequently attended as

spectators. These extraordinary exhibitions sank into disuse with the dissolution of the monasteries, but only to give place to others of a different description, till finally the procession of Godiva at the show fair became predominant, and has retained its fascinating hold on the minds of the inhabitants, and thousands of others, up to the present day, and appears likely to continue so to do; for although a strenuous effort was made so lately as the year 1845, by the whole clergy of the City, and the major part of the municipal authorities, backed up by a remonstrance from the Bishop of the Diocese, against the continuance of an usage alleged to be of so questionable a character, and so much at variance with the spirit of the age,—all this resistance failed to defeat the popular resolution which had been taken to enforce the procession as usual. On this occasion, however, the style of the procession was so good as to afford no reasonable ground for objection to the observance of this ancient usage.

Until the passing of the Municipal Reform Act, the procession of Godiva at Coventry fair was customarily graced by the full-robed attendance of the mayor and corporation. The presence of the civic body, however, has of late years been superseded by a fictitious substitute, and by the introduction of many new, but very suitable personations, namely, Edward the Black Prince; King Henry the 6th, and his Queen, Margaret of Anjou; Sir Thomas White; Sir William Dugdale the Warwickshire Historian; William and Adam Botoner, &c. &c.

The following is the Order of Procession, as constituted on those occasions when the Civic Body used to give it their patronage and attendance:— Captain of the Guards.
Chief of the Guards.
Two Lieutenants.
City Guards, marching two and two.
ftamt *George, in* armour.
Bugle Horns.
First City Streamer.
Two City Followers.
Second City Streamer.
Grand Band of Music.

The Chief Constable.
City Crier. L&IDY Beadle.
The City Bailiffs (two).
Mayor's Crier and Little Mace Bearer.
Bearers of the Great Sword and Mace.
THE MAYOR OF THE CITY.
Mayor's Followers (two).
The crrr Aldermen And Sheriffs.
Sheriffs' Followers (two).
Common Council and Chamberlains of the City.
Chamberlains' Followers.
Wardens.
Wardens' Followers.
Grand Band of Music.
Drums and Fifes.
ANCIENT COMPANIES OF THE CITY.
Mercers' Company.
Streamer, Master, and Followers.
DRAPERS.
Streamer, Master, and Followers.
Clothiers.
Streamer, Master, and Followers.
BLACKSMITHS.
Streamer, Master, and Followers.
TAILORS. Streamer, Master, and Followers. Grand Band of Music. Drums and Fifes. CAPPERS.
Streamer, Master, and Followers.
WEAVERS.
Streamer, Master, and Followers.
BUTCHERS.
Streamer, Master, and Followers.
FELLMONGERS.
Streamer, Master, and Followers. Grand Band of Music. Drums and Fifes.
CARPENTERS.
Streamer, Master, and Followers.
CORDWAINERS.
Streamer, Master, and Followers.
BAKERS.
Streamer, Master, and Followers.
SILK WEAVERS.
Streamer, Master, and Followers.
FULLERS.
Streamer, Master, and Followers.
Grand Band of Music. Drums and Fifes. Here follows, in continuation of the procession, a long and interesting array, consisting of the various Benefit Societies held at different houses in the City, each club introducing its own streamer, flag, or other insignia, together with two or more followers; and as there is a natural inclination on the part of these so-

cieties to do themselves credit in the pageant, they generally show a high degree of liberality, and conduce largely to the magnitude of the cavalcade. The orders of Odd Fellows and Foresters have lately been the most imposing feature among the clubs, sparing no expense in order to give conspicuous effect to the position they take in the procession. Last of the Societies comes that of the WOOL COMBERS.

Streamer, Master, and Followers.

SHEPHERD AND SHEPHERDESS,

In Rural Car of Green Boughs and Flowers, with Dog and Lamb.

Jason, with a Golden Fleece and Drawn Sword.

WOOL SORTERS.

Bishop Blaize.

Wool Combers, in appropriate Uniforms.

Grand Band of Music.

A fine copper-plate Engraving (price fid.) of the Procession, as above described, may be bad of the Booksellers where this work is sold; and a more minute Enquiry into the Origin and Character of this Exhibition has recently been published by Mr. D. Lewin, of Hertford-street, price 6d.

To this City, Leofric and the Countess Godiva were unquestionably great benefactors. The former died on the 2nd September, 1057, and was buried in a porch of the Monastery. The time of his lady's death is not exactly known, but she is stated to have been interred in another porch of the Monastery Church which they had founded. A record of the estates which they possessed in this County appears in Doomsday Book, which was compiled at the command of William the Conqueror, between the years 1081 and 1086.

THE MANOR OP CHEYLESMORE AND PARK.

With the citizens of Coventry, many reasons existed for holding in remembrance the names of Godiva and her powerful Lord; for to their protection, and that of their immediate descendants, they were indebted for much of the consequence which this City acquired in its early history. Shortly after the conquest, the lordship of Coventry devolved by

the marriage of Lucia, grand-daughter of Leofric, with Randolph de Meschines, to the Earls of Chester, who had a fortified mansion or castle within the Manor of Cheylesmore, on the south side of the town.

In the charter made by Hugh Kevelioc, Earl of Chester, to the Monks of Coventry, in the time of Henry the 2nd, pointing out the boundaries, and dividing the Earl's part from the Prior's, he traces it from St. Michael's church-yard, " nearly to the broad-gate of my castle." These were his words; and as " Broad Gate" is sufficiently well known now, it proves that the circuit of the outer ward of the castle was of great extent. In this family, and its collateral branches, the lordship remained till the reign of Edward the 3rd, when, on its falling to the crown, the King having advanced his son Edward the Black Prince to the dukedom of Cornwall, settled upon him this lordship, then called the Manor of Cheylesmore, annexing it to the dukedom for ever. Many privileges were afterwards bestowed upon this place. Edward the 3rd, in 1345, granted to his Queen, Isabel, during her life, and to the Prince and his heirs, in reversion, a court leet within this manor, with power to adjudge such cases as were generally taken before the Judges of Assize for the County of Warwick; they were empowered also to have a return of writs, relating to the good of felons and fugitives, within the district; and likewise to erect a gaol for the custody of felons.

At this time also a license was granted to Thomas de Quinton, to be keeper of the Park pasturage, on payment of *£5* annually, and *reserving sufficient grass for the deer.*

About the year 1388, several roods of land were separated from the Great Park and called the Little Park; and hence, no doubt, originated the names of the present " *Much"* and " *Little"* Park streets.

Here it is necessary to observe, that under the act for the redemption of the land tax, which was passed in the year 1798, in the reign of George III., his late Majesty George IV., when Prince of Wales, sold the Manor of Cheylesmore to the Marquis of Hertford, by whom

the beautiful avenues of trees in the Park were cut down, and what had been a pleasurable and healthful promenade for the inhabitants, ultimately became a vast enclosure of separate fields and gardens.

How the Manor and Park of Cheylesmore became the *disposable* property of the late George the Fourth, when Prince of Wales, or at least how it became alienated from the Corporation of Coventry, does not very clearly appear from any public record. For although after the death of John Eltham, Earl of Corne wall, Edward III. conferred upon his son Edward, called "the Black Prince," and *his heirs,* the reversion of the Dukedom of Cornwall, after the decease of Queen Isabel; yet *in default of such issue, it reverted to the Crown.* Edward VI. in 1549, by letters patent, dated July 19, granted Cheylesmore, with the Park, to John, Duke of Northumberland, and his heirs, as being part of the possessions annexed to the Duchy of Cornwall by charter. This Duke on the 12th of August following, made a lease of the premises to the Mayor, Bailiffs, and Commonalty of this City, for 99 years, upon the following conditions, viz., that they and their successors should pasture annually in the Park 80 cows or heifers, and 20 geldings, belonging to the poor inhabitants of the City, and that they should pay for every cow or heifer one penny, and for every gelding two-pence. But after the attainder of Northumberland, which happened in 1553, the Mayor, Bailiffs, &c, through the mediation of Robert, Earl of Leicester, obtained a grant from Queen Elizabeth, in 1568, to hold the above premises to them and their successors *for ever,* in fee farm, under several stipulations, the reserved rent of which was £9 per annum. On this subject the reader is referred to the inscription on a brass plate, now in St. Mary's Hall, which will confirm the account above given.

There are still some remnants of the Manor-house standing in Cheylesmore. It is entered by a large gateway in the front, which is of timber framework. The buildings on the eastern side are in many parts raised upon stone walls of great strength: but a close investigation is necessary to discover the few traces of its former importance.

THE GREAT FAIR.

Early in the reign of Henry III. was granted by that monarch, a charter for a yearly fair, to continue eight days, commencing on *the Friday in Trinity meek.* After the institution of this fair, it continued to be one of the principal marts in the kingdom, and was much frequented for the purchase of articles of general consumption, but especially for cloth, the manufacture of which was then extensively carried on in Coventry: and this fair still continues to be one of much celebrity and importance, greatly heightened in interest when the procession of Godiva forms an accompaniment to it.

THE CITY WALLS AND GATES.

The intestine disorders which often occurred about the period now under notice, and which, being calculated to impede the exertions of industry, rendered fortified barriers necessary to the security and protection of the trader in his transactions, and in the repository of his goods. In the 2nd of Edward III. the inhabitants were therefore empowered to assess and collect a tax towards defraying the expense of enclosing their town ' with a wall of lime and stone." This work, however, was not commenced till twentyseven years after the grant was obtained.

Towards the expense of fortifying the town, a license was granted to the citizens, empowering the Corporation to levy and collect, for five years, a duty of 2s. for every tun of wine sold in the town, 4d. for every quarter of malt, 4d. for every ox, Id. for every hog and calf, and for every sheep a farthing. Upon a complaint subsequently made by the publicans, they were eventually exempted from payment of these duties. Many years were devoted to the completion of these walls, with their towers, gates, and embattlements. They were three miles in circumference, and nine feet in thickness. Thirty-two towers, suited to purposes of defence, were set up at different points, and the twelve

gates were—New-gate, Gosford-gate, Mill Lane or Bastil-gate, Cook Street-gate, Bishop-gate, Well Street-gate, Hill Street-gate, Spon-gate, Grey Friars'-gate, Cheylesmoregate, and Little Park Street-gate.

These massive ramparts were kept in good repair for nearly 300 years; and some idea may be formed of the security they afforded to the City, by the defiance returned on the part of the inhabitants to the mandates of Edward IV. and Charles I., when those monarchs appeared before the gates with an armed force.

The following extracts from the old leet book of the Corporation, relative to the defence and guarding of the City in the troublesome times of Henry 6th and Charles 1st, will be read with interest. In 1448 the different companies of the City enrolled 603 men for its defence, who were provided with 683 jakkes or harburjons, salettes, bows, arrows, &c. 1449—Richard Sharp, Mayor, "Also, hit is ordeyned at ye p'sent lete, at the request & dosyr of ye Chamb'leyns, that ther shuld be ordeyned & named in ev'y warde iiij p'sones, which shuld have ye kepying & guyding of ye town yate: & they iiij in ev'y ward to chese on p'son, which shuld have ye kepying of ye keyes of ev'y yate, & he to open ye yate ev'y mornyng, & to lok hit at ix of ye clok in ye nyght: and they yt kept ye keyes of ye Newe-yate, Spon-Strete-yate, Byshop-yate & Frere-yate & Gosford-yate, to have yerely for ther labour iiij,s a pece; and they yt kept ye keyes-of all ye other yates, to have ij-s a pece, and to be paide be the Chamb'leyns for ye tyme beyng."

"1450—Hit is ordeyned (by the Mayor, Richard Boys, and 89 worthy men of the City, assembled in St. Mary's Hall,) for the wele of the Cite, that ye town dyches shnllon be clansed, and that to do, every howseholder of this Cite shall fynde a man, howse be howse, in lykewyse as the wache gothe, except that every wurthy man shall be charged to kepe ther parte also wel as odor.

"Also, they ordeyned, that portooles shull be made at ev'y yate of this Cite, ther as the yate is made to have a por-

tooles, and this to be don be the Chamburleyns of this Cite, atte Cite cost. Also, they ordeyned, that ther shuld be made Spayers witheín the water of Shirburn, to holde up the water yif nede requyre, and to lat ye passe all odur tymes, and this also to be don be the Chamburlens on the Cite coste.

"Also, that ther shuld be dyvers cheynes made of iron, and hanked in dyvers places withene this Cite, for to hang outhewarde dyvers lane endes, as hit now apereth where; and thys also to be don be over syht of the Meyr and his Councell.

"Also, that ther shuld be made a poaturne at the over partie of the Spon-strete, the which posturne shall be made atte costes of the seyde Spon-strete, that is to say, fro Bablake-yat upwards into the subarbs."

These chains were hung up at the ends of West-orchard, Broad-gate, Grey Friars'-lane, Pepper-lane, Little Park-street, Hay-lane, Bayley-lane, Much Park-street, and Dead-lane. Four pieces of ordnance were likewise purchased from Bristol, for the defence of the City, which, with the ammunition, &c, were placed in a tower in Bablake-gate.

"Jan.22,1642.—Christopher Davenport, Mayor. (From the Common Council book of the Corporation). Agreed, for the better defence of the Citie, some great pieces of ordnance be ordered from Bristol or elawhere, and that every householder and person of ability of this Citie, shall find and provide himself with such a proportion of musketts compleatly furnished, so this City maie have in a reddyness, upon any suddaine occasion, at least five hundred musketts for its defence and safeguard. To which end, there shall likewyse be provided with what convenient speed maie be, at the least, twentie musketts for the Corporation, to be in a rnadines in the armorie of the Citie, over and above the musketts the Citie now hath."

"*An Order touching Watch and Ward.*

"This House taking into consideration the present troubles and dangerous times, have, by the consent of the Com'on Council of this Cilie, thought fit and so order'd, that theire orders touching watch and ward Sri this Citie, shall be from henceforth duly kept and perform'd, and that delinquents shal be severely censured and punished, as enemys to the State.

"1st. That the watch shall everie night be set forth by the Alderman of the ward, or his deputie, at nine of the clock, and the watchmen to watch from that time till 5 of the clock the next morning.

"2nd. That no common or ordinarie watchmen be accepted or allowed of in theise troublesome times, but that the watch be perform'd by able men both of estate and persons.

"3rd. That one Common Councell man, and one other of this Citie that hath been Chamberlain or Warden, do duly oversee and observe the watch in this Citie, in the several wards and guards thereof.

"4th. That the Barr-gates be chained up everie night till 4 of the clock in the next morning, by the Alderman of the ward, or by his deputie, or a constable there.

"5th. That there be 17 men everie night imployed in the watch, to be disposed of thus: 3 at Spon-gate, 2 to walk in Spon-street, 3 at New-gate, 3 at Gosford-gate, 2 at Greyfriers-gate, 2 at Bishop-gate; theise 5 gates to be still attended with those watchmen, and the other 7 gates to be shut up everie night, and that 2 of those watchmen do everie night attend the Common Councell-men to walk the rounds.

"6th. The Gate at Crow Lane end, to be shut up everie night.

"7th. That speciall order be taken for the shutting up of the posterns gates, and the portcullis places in ye townwall, that no damage happen to the Citie."

"*Directions /or the Common Councell men and others the Chamberlains and Wardens, touching the Watch agreed upon to be had and Kept in this Cilie.* "1st. That they respectively do meete at the Maior's F'lor in Crosscheaping, at 9 of the clock, and that each of them as his turn cometh, viz. that one Com'on Councell man, one other person that hath been Chamberlain or Warden, and two constables and

two Watchmen do everie night walk the round of this Citie, to observe that the Watch do perform their dutie, and see that no danger or disorder be had in this Citie, and such walking the round to continue till *5* of the clock the next morning.

"2nd. That they see and observe that the gates and posterns appointed to be shut, be so ordered and kept in safetie.

"3rd. That the Com'on Councell men so walking the round, be ready the next morning to take in the weapons at the P'lor, that were overnyht deliver'd to them, and that they, so watching, do deliver to the Sheriffs notice where the Watch ended, to the end that from time to time the Sheriffs maie appoint who, by turn, are to supply that place of trust and care.

"4th. That this watch shall begin on Mondaie night the 24th of January, 1642, in Gosford-street ward, and 2 of the Constables there to watch the first night, and the next night one of that ward, and one of Much Park Street ward, till the whole Citie in each ward, has perform'd that service.

"5th. That those 2 Constables that last watched, are still from time to time, not only to give timely notice to the next 2 Constables who are by turn to watch, but also notice D to all other the inhabitants, who are by turne to watch, till each person in the ward have perform'd his and *her* dutie therein."

After the restoration, Charles II. resolved upon revenging himself for the hostility shown by Coventry to his father's cause, and determined upon razing its walls to the ground, although great pains had been taken on the part of the inhabitants to find favour and forgiveness from him.

On the 22nd of July, 1662, the Earl of Northampton, accompanied by some of the neighbouring gentry, and the City troops, made the first breach in the walls. Nearly five hundred men were occupied during three weeks and three days in the work of demolition, at the end of which time the greater part of the walls and towers were levelled; but most of the gates were left standing, and remained so till within the last century,

when at various times they were taken down, with the exception of three, which were of a subordinate character, and which have been permitted to go rapidly to decay. A considerable length of the wall, about eighteen feet high, standing near Gosford Bridge, was with great difficulty demolished by the aid of gunpowder so lately as the year 1814, and a row of tenements erected on its site. Several traces of the wall, however, may still be found. The most perfect portion of it is between the Cookstreet and Priory Gates.

INCORPORATION BY EDWARD III.

Coventry was indebted for many of its most distinguished privileges to Edward III. This monarch, in the year 1344, granted letters patent for constituting in the City a body Corporate, consisting of a Mayor and two Bailiffs, to be chosen annually by the inhabitants. Their patent also decreed that they should have power to settle all existing differences; that they should possess a common seal; and that a prison should be erected for the confinement of malefactors. In the 21st year of Edward III. John Ward became the first Mayor of this City.

CHARTER OF HENRY VI. "But above all the favours bestowed upon Coventry by former kings," says Dugdale, "that of King Henry VI., in the 30th of his reign, must have precedence; which king granted, that the said City, with the Villages and Hamlets of Radford, Keresley, Folkeshall, Eccleshale, Anesty, Calwedon, Wykene, Henley-la-Wode-End, Stoke, Byggyng, Whitteley, Pynley, Astbull, Horewell, Harnale, and Whaberley, as also part of Sow, and that part of Styvichale lying within the liberties of Coventre, all of which were within the precincts of the County of Warwick, should from the Feast of St. Nicholas (viz. 6th Dec.) next ensuing the date of his said Charter, be an entire County of itself, incorporate both in deed and name, distinct and altogether separate from the said County of Warwick forever, and no parcel of the same County; but from thenceforth called the County of the City of Coventry for ever. And that the Mayor and Bailiffs of the said City should thenceforth also for ever be elected at the same time and place, and according to the same manner and form, as they had used to be in the reign of King Edw. III. of famous memory, by virtue of his letters patent. And that the Bailiffs of the said City should be Sheriffs of the County of the said City for ever, still executing the office of Bailiffs as before."

The powers and jurisdiction established by this Charter of Henry VI. continued in existence until after the passing of the Municipal Reform Act in 1835, and the Amendment Act of a subsequent year.

BOUNDARIES OP COVENTRY—PAST AND PRESENT.

The ancient *inner* boundary of the City, exclusive of the suburbs, will have been sufficiently indicated by the situation of the several gates of the City Wall, as previously described.

Shortly after the passing of the Municipal Act, and Amendment Act, however, a protracted legal dispute arose between the Corporation, or Town Council, on the one side, and certain residents in some of the Hamlets and Villages forming part of the County of Coventry, under the Charter of Henry VI., on the other, which dispute was occasioned by the question as to the interpretation to be given to the term "City of Coventry," as used in the Acts above alluded to; it being concluded by the Corporation that such term included the City of Coventry *with its County,* as set out by the Charter of Henry VI., while the opponents of the Corporation held the reverse.

The contest on this question continued for several years. "Cases" were drawn up one after another on each side, and high legal "opinions" taken thereon, which opinions were so contradictory, or at least so little in unison with each other, that they only appeared to make "confusion worse confounded." Atlength, in the year 1842, the point was brought to a crisis, by an issue mutually agreed upon, to be argued by counsel on each side, before the Judges in the Court of Exchequer, who were thereupon to deliver their opinions; and on the 7th of July, in that year, judgment on the case was delivered at great length by Mr. Baron Parke, who concluded in

the following words:— "After fully considering the facts on both sides, and weighing their effect, we have come to the conclusion, that the 'Villa of Coventry' never did include within its ambit any of the parishes or places which are the subject of these issues."

Thus it will be seen that the Corporation-were nonsuited.

But although this decision settled the question, that certain parishes and hamlets were *not* part of the City of Coventry, it gave rise to another difficulty of a somewhat perplexing nature, by leaving the Magistrates and Corporation altogether in the dark as to what was the positive boundary, or to what extent they were authorized to exercise their jurisdiction and authority; and the same difficulty was felt by the Magistrates of the County of Warwick. The Corporation of Coventry therefore resolved to petition the Secretary of State, praying that a bill might immediately be submitted to Parliament, to incorporate Coventry with the County of Warwick; and accordingly an Act to that effect was promptly passed by the Legislature, and received the Royal Assent on the last day of the Session of 1842.

This measure extinguished the ancient offices of Recorder, Sheriffs, and Coroner of Coventry, and made an entirely new arrangement as to the holding of the Assizes and Sessions.

Under the provisions of this Act an order in Council was gazetted on the 3rd of February, 1843, forming the County of Warwick into two divisions, each having a separate commission of assize, namely, the "Warwick Division" and the "Coventry Division." The latter comprises the City of Coventry, together with the Atherstone and Coleshill Divisions of the Hundred of Hemlingford; and the Kirby and Rugby Divisions of the Knightlow Hundred. The Quarter Sessions are held in Coventry by adjournment from Warwick, the Chairman of the County Sessions presiding. The Act also assigned the following boundary for the City of Coventry:—

' From the point at which the Boundary of Trinity Parish crosses the

road from Coventry to Leicester, eastward and southward along the boundary of the said parish to the point at which it meets the boundary of the Parish of St. Michael, near the road from Coventry to Lutterworth; thence in a straight line to the point at which the northern fence of the land belonging to the London and Birmingham Railway Company meets the western bank of the River Sherbourn; thence westward along the said fence to the point at which the same crosses Elsdon-lane; thence northward along Elsdonlane to the point at which the same meets the southern boundary of Hearsall Common; thence in a straight line drawn due north to the point at which such straight line cuts the River Sherbourn; thence in a straight line to the point at which the lane which leads from the Radford Road to Saint Nicholas-lane leaves the Radford Road; thence along the said lane to the point at which the same meets Saint Nicholaslane; thence in a straight line drawn due east to the point at which such straight line cuts the

Canal; thence northward along the Canal to the next bridge, being the second bridge across the said Canal; thence eastward along the road leading from the said bridge to the road from Coventry to Leicester; thence along the said road to the point first described."

The above boundary having been duly set out, is now marked by sixteen meer stones, which are placed in the following situations, and have the letters C. C. cut therein:— *Western Boundary.* —1, Elsdon Lane; 2, Northern fence of Hearsall Common; 3, Old Birmingham Road.; 4, River Sherbourn; 5, New Birmingham Road; 6, Barker's Butts Lane; 7, Radford Brook; 8, bottom of St. Nicholas Lane; 9, top of St. Nicholas Lane; 10, Sandy Lane; 11, Canal Bank. *Eastern Boundary.*—12, Jabet's Ash; 13, Southern fence of Gosford Green; 14, Folly Lane; 15, Footpath to Pinley; 16, Boundary of the London and Birmingham Railway.

K fttonagtic Institutions.

THE PRIORY.

"*The famous Monastery*" for the maintenance of twenty-four monks and an abbot of the order of St. Benedict, was, as has been previously stated, founded in 1044, by Leofric and Godiva, on the ruins of the great Convent which had been destroyed some years before, by Edric the Traitor.

In an account given by Dugdale relative to this order of monks, and their habits, he says,— "Benedict assign'd to his monks a special kind of habit, and appointed them a certain form for praying, slender diet, and a new rule of abstinence; and that except in case of sickness, they should wholly forbear flesh. Which monks of St. Benedict's rule, as their tradition is, do wear a black coat loose and divided down to their heels, with a cowl or hood for their head, that falling over their shoulders, is shorter than others use: and under all, have a woollen white coat, as also a hair shirt, with boots to the knees, their heads being shaved with a razor below the midst. "

This monastery was endowed with vast wealth, for it is related that Earl Leofric, " by the advice and licence of King Edward the Confessor, and Pope Alexander, at the dedication of the church to the honour of God and his blessed Mother, as also of *St. Peter* the Apostle, and the Holy Virgin *St. Osburg,* and *All-Saints,* did give, besides the one-half of this town, in which the said monastery was situate, twenty-four lordships for maintenance of the abbot and monks, there serving God, with food and raiment," &c, and to this were superadded many other immunities.

The office of Abbot, however, in the course of a few years was superseded, in consequence of the government of the monastery falling into the bands of the Bishop of the Diocese, which then comprised Chester, Coventry, and Lichfield; for although there were Abbots occasionally afterwards, they were but mere delegates of the Bishop. The first Bishop who took upon himself the government, seems to have had little regard for the institution of which he had become the head. Dugdale thus speaks of him:— "This Bishop was neither a friend to the Monastery nor to the Monks; for besides his scraping so

much silver from the beams, he suffered the buildings to go to decay, pill'd the church of many rich ornaments; and as for the poor Monks, he kept them so poor and miserable, not regarding their regular living, nor anything that might advance learning among them: to the end that being thus brought low, and in ignorance, their thoughts should not soar so high as to consider the redress of these his so great injuries."

The same historian then recites the names of a number of Bishops, " all which," says he, "in their severall times successively, did stile themselves *Coventriw Episcopi* only; and had a fair Palace at the north-east corner of St. Michael's Church Yard, being very near to the said Monastery."

But after the sad condition to which the monastery was reduced as above described, it rallied again and rose to augmented power and splendour, though not without occasional conflicts and reverses. The particulars of these events are given at length by Sir W. Dugdale, who thus concludes his account:—" But behold the instability of these terrestriall things; what the pious founder, and all other its worthy benefactors, had with great zeal to God's glory, so cheerfully given and bestowed on the structure, endowment, and adorning of this sometime famous monastery; and that with such heavy imprecations and curses upon any that should take away or diminish ought thereof, as the charters do manifest; against which violators of the Church its patrimony, the representative body of this realm had also, so often, *in terrorem,* pronounc't solemn curses in open Parliament, (as whosoever shall cast his eye upon her statutes and publique history may discern:) was subverted, torn away, and scattered in 30th of King Henry 8th's reign, after it had stood near 500 years, the glory of all these parts: at which time the very Church itself, though a most beautifull Cathedkall, and the motherchurch of this City, scap't not the rude hands of the destroyers; but was pull'd in pieces and reduc't to rubbish. For the countenance of which sad act, the then Prior and Covent, seeing the fate of some oth-

ers that refus'd, was no less than to be hang'd up at their gates, were brought to make surrender of the same into the hands of the Commissioners for the King's use, as appears by their public seal bearing date 15 January in the year abovesaid."

Then follows the names of the prior and monks who subscribed the capitulation to the 40 Bishop's Palace—Bemains Op Cathedral. king, and who received pensions for their respective lives as the reward of their degradation and subjection.

The annual revenues of this monastery at the time of its dissolution is recorded by Dugdale as being £731. 19s. 5d.

The scite of this building, with its messuages, gardens, mills, &c, was soon afterwards granted to John Coombes and Richard Stansfield, from whom it descended into the hands of John Hales (of whom further notice will occur in subsequent pages).

Whilst this monastery, with its cathedral, &c, were standing, Coventry could boast of a matchless group of ecclesiastical buildings, extending, as the small remains still show, from what is now the lower part of the Great Butcherrow to the bottom of the north side of St. Michael's Church-yard, where a tenement called "Bishop's Palace" yet stands. The cathedral, supposed to have been on a model of that at Lichfield, stood in a place called Hill Close, on a gentle declivity from the north side of St. Michael's and Trinity Church-yards. The present Dog public-house in the Butcher-row, stands on the scite of a stately gateway which led to the Close. Many fragments of this magnificent pile of building, plainly REMAINS OF CATHEDRAL—OREY FRIARS. 41 indicating the doorways of the monks' residences, may still be seen in the vicinity of "Hill Top," as well as down the "Wood-yard" at the top of New Buildings, on which spot these vestiges of antiquity, (as shewn in the annexed sketch,) have recently been rendered more visible by the clearance made in the pulling down of a range of butchers' stables. The scite of the cathedral church was in 1776 consecrated anew, as an additional burying place for Trinity Parish.

THE GREY FRIARS. The Grey Friars sprung from St. Francis, an Italian. Matthew of Westminster says, "They were diligent instruments for the Pope in all his affaires, sometimes as messengers or legates, It may be necessary here to state, that the small wood cuts introduced in this work are copied from a series of medals representing various public buildings in Coventry, which were struck many years ago; and this explanation will account for any discrepancies which may be noticed between these engravings and the *present* appearance of some of the objects represented. sometimes in gathering up taxes, alwaies sedulous for his advantage: neither were they slack in preaching, signing with the cross, and assisting the sick in making of their testaments. As to their habits, they were decidedly of a mendicant order, living wholly on charity, going about in couples, with wallets on their shoulders, to collect almes." The settlement of this order in Coventry must have been in the former part of the 13th century; and their monastery and church were built by charitable contributions, on a spot of ground given to them by Randal, the last Earl of Chester, out of his neighbouring Manor of Cheylesmore. The Grey Friars' Monastery at Coventry was amongst the last which fell a prey to the rapacity of Henry 8th, who compelled the friars to sign and seal their own surrender. The remains and scite of this house, including the handsome spire of its church, were in 1542 granted by the same monarch to the Mayor, Bailiffs and Commonalty of Coventry, and their successors for ever.

On the south-east part of this City stood the Monastery of the White Friars, or Carmelites, another sort of mendicants, who made their appearance in England about the year 1250. It was not, however, till nearly a century afterwards that they settled in Coventry; the house here having been built for them by Sir John Poultney, Knight, Lord Mayor of London. They are spoken of as having won so much of the esteem of the people

by their strict rule of living, that few persons of quality residing within many miles, failed, in their testaments, to give liberally to them. Their Monastery in Coventry was considerably enlarged in the year 1419, by the gift of William Botener, of Withibroke.

Upon the survey made by Henry VIII., the clear annual value of this house was *SH.* 13s. 8d.; and in 1558 these poor friars were compelled to follow the example of others, and made surrender to the King, being turned adrift without pension or allowance of any kind.

F

The Monastery, with its revenues, except an annual payment of 20s. to Merton's Charity, was granted to Sir Ralph Sadler, from whom it descended to John Hales, who made it his residence; from him the house descended, through various hands, to the Rev. Mr. Smith, of Apsley, Bedfordshire, who sold it in 1801 to the Directors of the Poor in this City, by whom it was converted into a Workhouse, or House of Industry.

There are extensive remains of this Monastery yet standing, which offer much that is worthy of inspection; for, although intersected in various ways by modern additions to meet the purposes to which it is now devoted, many parts of the ancient structure still exist in a good state of preservation, particularly of the arched cloisters, the dormitory, and refectory, and the old gateway in the garden (see wood-cut below). The outer-gateway may still be seen in Much Park-street, where it forms the entrance to White Friars'-lane.

THE CARTHUSIAN MONASTERY OR CHARTER HOUSE.

The Carthusian Monastery formerly stood on the south-east side of the City, and its existing remains are now known by the name of "The Charter House."

The order of Carthusians sprung from one Bruno, a learned man, and a native of Germany, in the year 1080, and was first introduced into England by Henry II. towards the close of the twelfth century. This religious house, in Coventry, originated with William Lord Zouch, of Harringworth, in Northamptonshire, in 1381, who, however, died before he had

fully executed his purpose, but left by will £60 per annum towards the establishment; and the design was afterwards carried out by various persons, commencing with Richard Luff, a Mayor of Coventry, and John Botener, a fellow-citizen, who bestowed four hundred marks on the church, choir, cloisters, and three cells on the east side next to the Chapter House; and for the purpose of excavating seven ponds for water. By subsequent benefactions these cells were augmented in number, and the establishment further enlarged and beautified.

In the year 1385 Richard II., on his return from Scotland, assumed the honour of being the founder of this house, and laid the first stone of the church, declaring, in the presence of the Mayor and Citizens of Coventry, that he would bring it to perfection. After this, it received considerable endowments, and at the dissolution was found, according to Dugdale, to be possessed of £131. 6s. 8d. per annum, free of all deductions. In 1538 it was surrendered to Henry VIII. by the Prior and eight Monks, the Prior being rewarded with a pension of *£40* a year.

The monks of this order appear to have led a rigid and self-denying life. Their cells were built with a low roof, and contained three or four rooms on the ground floor; behind which was a little garden with a high wall; and into these cells the lay brethren introduced their food through a little door in the wall, which was locked, the key being kept by the person who served them. No women were allowed to enter the liberties of the monastery.

Although the outer-wall of the precinct is standing, little of the ancient building remains. In the garden, however, are the marks of many small doors, and traces of the entrances into the cells of their former austere inhabitants.

THE CROSS.

"Thy mouldering Cross, with ornament profuse,

Of pinnacles and niches proudly rais'd,

Height above height, a sculptur'd chronicle."

Jago's Edge Hill. "Cross Cheaping" derives its name from the original cross, which was set up there in the year 1423, and was taken down in 1510.

In the year 1541 another Cross was commenced, and was completed in 1544, it having been founded by Sir William Hollies, Knight, once Lord Mayor of London, and son to Thomas Hollies, of Stoke, near to this City. This gothic pile was sexagonal; each side seven feet at the base, finely diminishining, pyramidically, in three stories, fifty-seven feet high, with eighteen niches. The canopy was beautifully adorned with statues, some of which had been brought from the White Friars. The pillars, pinnacles, and arches, were enriched with a variety of figures, and with flags, on which were displayed the arms of England, or the Rose of Lancaster; representations were also added of the founder, trades, and companies; and the whole was so finely finished, that it was inferior to none in England for exquisite workmanship and beauty.

On the summit of the uppermost story was the figure of Justice; in the upper story, St. Peter, St. James, and St. Christopher; second story, Edward III., St. Michael, Henry III., St. George, and Richard II.; in the lower story, Henry VI., King John, Edward I., Henry II., Richard I., and Henry V.

In 1669 the Cross was thoroughly repaired, and so highly decorated with painting, gilding, &c, that it became the admiration of the times. Such was the splendid appearance of this Cross at that time, that it was said "it's lustre was almost too bright to look upon." From this period it was totally neglected, and by the gradual operation of the weather, mouldered away and decayed, until the year 1771, when the remains of this once splendid pile were wholly removed. One of the figures from the niches, supposed to be the statue of Henry VI., in good preservation, is now standing near the foot of the staircase leading into Saint Mary's Hall.

SPON HOSPITAL OR CHAPEL.

"The Chapel or Hospital of Sponne," as Dugdale describes it, was founded in Henry H.'s time, by Hugh Keveliok, Earl of Chester, who, having a certain knight of his household who was a leper, established and endowed this Hospital for the maintenance of such lepers as should happen to be in the town of Coventry. Here were anciently resident at least one priest to celebrate divine service for the living and the dead; and with him had also wont to be certain brethren and sisters, together with the lepers, praying to God for all their benefactors.

This Hospital fell into the hands of the crown at the same time with the Manor of Cheylesmore; but in the reign of Edward IV. it was passed away, with its revenues, to the Canons of Studley and their successors, in pure alms, to pray for the good estate of the king and his queen during their lives; and for their souls, and the souls of several other distinguished people, after death.

The old stone gateways, now converted into tenements, near to Spon-end Bridge, are the only vestiges of this Hospital which are to be seen at the present time.

Of all the remnants of antiquity which this city retains, the Hospital now under notice is unquestionably that which has had preserved to it its primitive form and exterior with the smallest amount of innovation. Its situation is in Grey Friars'-lane; it having been founded in the year 1529 by William Ford, a merchant of Coventry, and its endowment further increased by William Pisford, his executor, whose will (too long for insertion here) contains some remarkable details of the objects to which his benevolence was devoted. The Hospital is a very curious timber building, surrounding a court-yard equally singular for its ancient appearance. It contains a number of apartments for the inmates, as well as rooms and offices for other purposes connected with the establishment.

I (1

Perhaps a finer specimen of the domestic English architecture of the sixteenth century is not to be found anywhere, than this Hospital presents.

It was originally founded for the reception of aged married couples, "of good name and fame," inhabitants of Coventry; and was afterwards strengthened in its resources by many benefactors. This excellent institution now affords a comfortable retreat, and security from want, to aged females alone, of whom there are eighteen or twenty, besides a nurse to administer to their wants. Each inmate receives 3s. 6d. per week, and coal for use. There are also about twenty-five out-door recipients of the same weekly amount of money, and a ton of coals annually. A rule has been adopted by the trustees for some years past that no one shall be admitted who has ever received parochial relief; and in several instances parties have been excluded on being discovered to have gained admission in contravention of this regulation.

The present revenue of this hospital is upwards of £500 per annum, from which however some deductions have to be made for repairs and other charges.

Q dish their meat and drink, and who by his will directed that they should have "every year a gown of black, with a hood, and that they be every day at the beginning of mattins, mass, and evening song." That the said ten men should be bounden " daily, after they have supped, to go into the church, and there kneeling, every man to say fifteen paternosters and fifteen aves, and three greeds, in the worship of the passion of Christ, and then to drink and go to bed."

Succeeding donors considerably augmented the funds of this charity, the revenues of which now amount to upwards of £1,000 a-year; but of course the lapse of time, together with the course of events, has essentially changed the character of the religious duties required to be performed by the alms-men, of whom there are about forty-five, resident and non-resident, each of whom receives 6s. per week, and is, on occasion of attending divine service at church, attired in the black gown originally ordained.

The building, which had been suffered to fall into a wretched state of dilapidation, was some years ago thoroughly and substantially repaired, and now forms a most comfortable abode for its aged domestics. This hospital, although perhaps less picturesque as a memorial of antiquity, possesses the substantial advantage of being much more commodious as a dwelling place, than the women's hospital in Grey Friar's lane. The rooms of the old men are decidedly airy and pleasant, and are approached by long corridors, convenient for health and in-door exercise. Each inmate has also a small piece of ground assigned to him in the large garden, which is a sort of promenade; and there is a common kitchen as a sitting room, at all times open. It is a remarkable fact that by the decisions of the revising barristers under the Parliamentary Reform Act, the Bablake-men enjoy a vote for the County *as freeholders,* although such of them as are freemen of Coventry, are disqualified from voting for the City, in consequence of being reputed as *almsmen.*

St. John's Hospital, for the reception of the sick and needy, was founded by Lawrence, a Prior of Coventry, about the year 1155, and the Friars belonging thereto, and received many benefactions in the time of Henry II. and subsequent reigns. Its annual income at the time of the general survey was valued at £99. 13s. 6d., when it was of course dissolved under Henry VIII., who, Dugdale says, "granted it, (for a small consideration) with all the lands and possessions thereunto belonging, unto John Hales, Gent., and his heirs: which John, being an active man in those days, and Clerk to the Hamper (an office then of no small benefit), and he, having accumulated a great estate in Monastery and Chantry-lands, resolved to erect a. lasting monument to his memory (for he had neither child nor wife), and thereupon, designing the foundation of a Free School here, converted the buildings to that purpose, dedicating the same to Henry VIII."

The founder of this school died in 1573, and by his will directed his executors to convey to the Mayor, Bailiffs, and Commonalty of Coventry the scite of the hospital and lands, with messuages, &c, lying in Coventry, (belonging to the late dissolved Priories of Coventry and Kenilworth,) together with the White Friars', Bastille, and Hill Mills, to the intent that out of the rents of the said property the annual sum of £20 should be paid to a schoolmaster, to teach grammar in the school, £10 to an usher, £2. 12s. to a music master, to instruct every scholar who should be willing to learn to sing, three times every week, and *£1.* 6s. 8d. per annum to a bailiff to collect the rents and see that the houses were kept in good repair: the residue to be employed in reparing the above houses, and augmenting the salaries of the schoolmaster and usher, the former of whom it was ordained should have for his habitation the mansion-house wherein the master of the said hospital did dwell, and the usher to reside in another house within the scite of the said hospital.

It would appear from existing documents, that John Hales first established this school at the Church of the White Friars, where the scholars sat in the seats of the choir; but it being subsequently discovered that, although he had bought the lands, he had not bought the church, a grant from the Crown was obtained, whereby the church was ordered to be pulled down; and Mr. Hales removed the scholars and the seats to their present situation. The front of the school was pulled down in 1794, for the purpose of widening the street. On digging the foundation for the new front, which, however, is now (1847) in a sad state of decay, the base and part of a pillar, much older than any part of the present structure, were discovered. The chapel of the Hospital, now reduced to little more than a portion of one aisle, is the present school, and the ancient oak seats with which it is still fitted up are remarkable specimens of the workmanship of the olden time.

Connected with this school used to be a large and valuable library, but which has now become much mutilated. Particulars of the manner in which this school was at one time managed under corporation trusteeship, will be found in the Charity Commissioners' Reports; and although it was decidedly improved during the latter time of the late corporation, and further since placed under the control of new trustees, there is still too much ground for the general complaint of the inhabitants, that it is a comparatively exclusive institution. Its revenues and expenditure, according to the Corporation Commissioners' Report, published about 12 years ago, stood as follows:— *£. 8. d.*

Rental of the Estates belonging to the School 890 4 5

Expenditure.—The Head Master 525 13 3

The Under Master 262 16

The Singing Master 4 0 0

Repairs 19 0 0

Bailiff's Salary 43 0 0

Incidental Expenses.... 8 6 6

Loss by Insolvency, &c. 27 8 Of £890 4 5

The present Head Master is the Rev. T. Sheepshanks, the Second Master the Rev. W. Drake, who also, in accordance with an Act of Parliament, hold respectively, in conjunction therewith, the first the Rectorship, and the second the Lectureship of St. John's Church.

The ancient gilds were formed of fraternities of merchants and others, who "were either for charity, religion, or merchandise sake, associated, and did cast their moneys, goods, yea, and sometimes lands, together, for the public support of their own common charge. These had their annuall feasts and neighbourlike meetings, to which the country people were occasionally invited, and became partakers of the common bounty."

Of such gilds there were several in Coventry, viz., Merchants' Gild, Trinity Gild, Corpus Christi Gild, Sheremen and Tailor's Gild, and St. Katharine's Gild. To the latter belonged that stately structure St. Mary's Hall, opposite the south side of St. Michael's Church, a noble edifice which has been well preserved, and is eminently worthy of notice. This Hall was founded about the beginning of Henry 6th's time, and still presents an extraordinary piece of evidence as to the wealth and importance of the merchants resident in this town and neighbourhood in past ages, and of the magnificence which marked the character of their fraternal proceedings.

In entering the court-yard of the Hall, *the Gateway first* demands attention. In this porch, on the key-stone of the arch, is a basso-relievo, representing God on his throne receiving St. Mary, who is sitting with her hands joined in the attitude of prayer. On a projecting stone, now fast mouldering away, is sculptured the Annunciation, though the figures of St. Mary and the Angel are still discernible, as also a flower-pot in the centre. The corresponding stone in the opposite abutment is wrought with grotesque animals. Passing through the courtyard into *the Kitchen,* the immense fire-places and huge coppers at once indicate the liberal scale on which the entertainments of these Gilds were conducted. Entering next into the basement story, or *Cellar* of the Hall, the doorways, windows, columns, groins, and sculptures, prove the exalted ideas and fervour of imagination which marked the undertakings of the architects of former times.

B

The Great Hall is a fine old room, 21 yards long and 10 yards broad, with a beautiful timber roof altogether unsupported by pillars or arches. In the timber-work of this roof will be found some most admirable whole-length carvings of angels playing on musical instruments, which are a crewth, trumpet, cittern, harp, and bass flute. The attitude of the performer on the harp is correct and exquisitely tasteful.

The object, however, which first attracts the eye, is the *noble Window of old Stained Glass* at the north end of the Hall. This window is divided into nine compartments, in which are figures of several of our monarchs, with coats of arms and ornaments. The arms now left are those of Kings Henry 6th, Edward 3rd, the Emperor Constantine, King Ethelred, the Earl of Cornwall, the Duke of Normandy, the Kingdom of the East Angles, the King9 of Man, the City of London, King Alfred, the Duke of Aquitaine, the City of York, and the Earl of Chester. Underneath are the figures of Kings William the Conqueror, Richard 1st, Henry 5th, Henry 4th, Emperor Constantine, Kings Arthur, Henry 3rd, and Henry 6th.

The east and west sides of the Hall are also ornamented, each with three beautiful windows of stained glass, but of modern quality. They are nevertheless very fine specimens of workmanship and art, and exhibit figures of a number of individuals whose names are connected with the ancient history of the town. Below the great north window is an exquisite piece of *Ancient Tapestry,* 10 feet in depth, and measuring the whole width of the hall. It is divided into six compartments, in two tiers, one above the other. In the first compartment (beginning from the left hand), will be noticed Henry 6th, with several of the principal nobility of his court. Henry is on his knees, and before him is a covered table, whereon lie his crown and a missal. Behind the King is Cardinal Beaufort, in the same attitude. The rest of the personages are standing. Taking in the whole group, the major part of them appear deeply impressed with their devotional exercises. In the compartment above are several of the Apostles. Here are likewise two Christian Knights. In the second compartment of the first tier is St. Mary in glory, surrounded by angels, with the moon under her feet. The attitude of this representation is chaste and elegant, and the robes are as appropriate as any human mind could devise, so as to combine earthly attire and heavenly array. On each side of St. Mary are the twelve Apostles, in devotional positions. In the compartment above are the heavens opened, and angels round the throne; but it is to be lamented that the original figure in the centre has been cut out (probably by some of the early reformers), and a poor effort of the loom—a figure of justice, sewed in its place. In the third compartment on the first tier are represented Margaret, Henry's consort, with a table and missal before her. Near the Queen is the Duchess of Buckingham, together with other ladies, including two nuns in the full habit of their order. The tier above shews many female saints, corresponding with the male saints on the opposite compartment of the tapestry, before described.

In the year 1580 the inside of the Hall was painted and beautified, and a variety of heraldic emblems and inscriptions set forth on oak wainscotting round the walls. These decorations were, with great fidelity to the originals, renewed about twenty years ago, but were most unfortunately and injudiciously painted merely on a coating of Roman cement. The consequence is, that with the exception of two or three at the upper end of the Hall, they have entirely disappeared, the obliteration having been much accelerated by the large assemblages of persons at public meetings, which of late years it has been customary to hold in this Hall, and the walls being altogether unprotected by any kind of fence.

In the Great Hall will be found a number of fine *Paintings,* comprising full-length representations of Charles II., James II., William and Mary, George I., George II. and Caroline, George III., and George IV.

The *Minstrel Gallery* is at the south end of the Hall, and at the front of this gallery, well arranged, and in good repair, is *the ancient City Armour,* which is particularly deserving of inspection. The *ancient Chair of State,* a massive piece of old oak furniture, standing in the Hall, and in which several English Kings and Queens have been occasionally seated, is also a remarkable relic of antiquity.

Underneath the Minstrel Gallery are the doorways leading to the old Council Chambers, apartments which will well repay the attention of the visitor.

The *Mayoress's Parlour,* situate on the east side of the great hall, with a doorway leading therefrom, was thoroughly repaired in the year 1835, and has now a comparatively modern appearance, although the style observed in the restoration of the interior approximates pretty much to that of the other parts of the structure. It is at present used as a police court by the City Magistrates. Upon the walls are suspended a fine whole-length portrait of Queen Anne, with half-lengths of Queen Mary, Queen Elizabeth, Charles I., James I., and of Sir Thomas White, and others of the City's benefactors, together with a fine painting of Lady Godiva on horseback.

The hall is the property of the Corporation, and an order to view it gratuitously may be obtained from any member of the Town Council.

DRAPERS' HALL.

This Hall is situate nearly opposite the lower door on the south side of St. Michael's Church. The original building of the name, a dismal and unsightly edifice, was pulled down in 1775, and another shortly afterwards erected on its site; but this in its turn, being extensively damaged by dry rot, was in 1830 removed, and in its stead the present structure was raised, after a design by Messrs. Rickman and Hutchinson, being finished and opened two years afterwards, viz., on the 8th of November, 1832. The architecture is of the Grecian style; and on the front are the arms of the Drapers' Company. The various compartments of this Hall are elegant, spacious, and convenient; and most of them are agreeably lighted by dome lights. There is a card room 20 feet square, a tea room 40 feet by 24 feet, and a ball room 60 feet by 30, in which is a small orchestra of a delightfully chaste character, splendid chandeliers, and costly mirrors at each end of the room. The building is chiefly devoted to the meetings and festive assemblings of the Drapers' Company, who, however, grant the use of the Hall occasionally to parties, and for purposes of which they approve, having a strict regard to the preservation of the property from injury; though there is some reason to fear that it is not altogether untouched by the inroads of the dry-rot, notwithstanding the great care with which it is attended to.

THE COUNTY HALL.

In the year 1785 was erected the County Hall, which formerly belonged to the Corporation of Coventry, but was transferred to the Magistracy of the County at large under the New Boundary Act, passed in 1842, and under the provisions of which the Corporation were ordered to be paid, by instalments, the sum of.£17,000 out of the county purse, that having been adjudged to be the value of the same, together with the Gaol and House of Correction adjoining.

This Hall, which has undergone considerable improvement in its internal arrangements since it became the property of the County, is, according to its dimensions, one of the best adapted in the kingdom for the transaction of assize and sessions business. It is built with a light-coloured stone, and has Roman Doric columns in front.

THE GAOL.

The Gaol stands in immediate connexion with the County Hall in front, and extends to some distance behind it. It was erected at a large cost nearly twenty years ago, when it was set out and constructed in conformity with the regulations of the Act of Parliament for the Building of Prisons, 4th Geo. 4, cap. 64. It comprises 84 cells, nearly the whole of which are single bedded; has nine separate yards, and eight separate day rooms. Since it became the property of the County at large, it has been chiefly appropriated for the retention of prisoners previous to trial: and her Majesty's Judges of Assize, and the Chairman of Quarter Sessions, in conformity to the views of the County Magistrates, almost invariably order that prisoners convicted, and sentenced to any term of imprisonment, shall be removed for that purpose to Warwick.

ST. MICHAEL'S CHURCH. It is questionable whether the entire kingdom supplies a finer architectural specimen, as a parish church, than that of St. Michael, Coventry, which still excites the admiration of i every visitor, as it has done for ages that are past. Dugdale says, " Of this church, the first mention that I find is in King Stephen's time (about the middle of the 12th century); for then did Ranulph, Earl of Chester, render it to the (Benedictine) Monks of Coventry, by the name of the Chappell of St. Michael, being satisfied by the testimony of divers persons, as well clergy as laytie, that it was their right. Which act of his, Earl Hugh, his son and successor confirmed. Hereunto also did Earl Ranulph, the last of that name, give the tythe of his lands and rents in Coventre, for the health of his soul, and of his ancestors' souls; commanding all his officers, upon pain of a grievous curse, to make due payment of them accordingly. What colour of right the bishop had in the advowson, I find not; but it seemes that a claime he made thereto; so that in 32 Henry 3, the Prior and he came to an agreement, whereupon the said Prior, to purchase the bishop's interest, parted with the perpetuall patronage of the Churches of Ryton and Bobenhull, then settling them upon the Cathedrall of Lichfield, whereof since that time they have been prebends. In anno 1291, 19 Edward 1st, this church, with its chappels, was valued at 50 marks; and the vicaridge at 8 marks and a half. The tall and beautifull steeple, which for its workmanship and height is inferior to none in England, was more than 22 years in building—being begun in 1373 and finished in 1395. But I find that in 12th Henry 6th (1434) there was a new work begun upon this church, yet what in particular I cannot directly say; howbeit, by the fashion of the building, do I conceive, that the whole body of the church, or the greater part thereof, was then built in that form we now behold it. In the 26th Henry 8 the vicaridge was rated at £65. 10s. 6d."

The steeple tower was erected by Adam and William Botoner, citizens, and several times Mayors of Coventry, and who for above 22 years expended £100 annually, *during the reign of Richard II,* (a large sum at that period,) in carrying on this magnificent work. The beautiful spire is said to have been finished by Ann and Mary Botoner, who also built the middle aisle of the church, a lofty structure 50 feet high.

The tower rises immediately from the ground, at the west end of the church. It is 136 feet 3 inches high from the base to the battlements. The windows of it are well proportioned; the buttresses fine, with ajust admixture of embossed carved work and embroidery; but unfortunately the ornamental details have become very indistinct, in consequence of the action of time on the soft stone of which the building consists. The niches of the upper part are furnished with thirty figures of the Roman saints, of good statuary. Upon this tower stands an octagonal prism, 32 feet 6 inches high, and supported by double flying buttresses of graceful construction, springing from the lower part of the four pinnacles of the first tower. From within the battlements of the octagonal tower issues the spire, 130 feet 9 inches high, adorned with curious fluting; and the walls of which are 17 inches thick at the bottom, and so exquisitely tapered as to recline but four and a half degrees from the perpendicular,—a finished piece of architecture which was pronounced by Sir Christopher Wren to be a masterpiece of art. The entire height of the tower and spire, from the base to the summit, is 303 feet.

It is said that while the steeple was in course of erection, *New-street* was built, consisting of small houses, as habitations for the workmen employed upon it.

The church is 293 feet 9 inches in length in the interior, and 127 feet in breadth, comprising nave, chancel, and two aisles equal in length with the nave, besides two shorter ones. The church is divided by rows of high and airy pillars and arches, of unparalleled elegance, with fine oaken roof, and the whole presents a grand and imposing aspect when viewed from a favourable point, which may be found at either end of the edifice. The windows are good, though not retaining any very great extent of the old stained glass of which they were originally formed.

This church is further distinguished by one of the best organs in the kingdom. It was originally erected in 1733, by Thomas Swarbrick, a German, and cost about £1,400, but has subsequently undergone extensive repairs and additional improvements, particularly in being for the most part rebuilt in 1836, at an expense of nearly £600, and under the inspection of its present talented organist, Mr. E. Simms.

The monuments are not very numerous, but there are, nevertheless, several which will be found worthy of notice, as also a variety of epitaphs and inscriptions, some of them highly curious and amusing, as for instance the following upon a brass plate in a slab, with the family arms, in the floor, at the west end of the church:—

"Here lyes the body of Capt. Gervase Scrope, of the family of Scrapes, of Bolton, in the County of York, who departed this life the 2Cth day of Aug., Anno Do'ni 1705, aged 60.

"An epitaph written by himself in the agony and dolorous paines of the gout, and died soon after.

"Here lyes an old toss'd Tennis Ball,
Was racketted from Spring to fall,
With so much heat and so much hast
Time's arm for shame grew tyr'd at last.
Four Kings in Camps he truly serv'd,
And from his honesty ne'er swerv'd.
Father ruin'd, the Son slighted,
And from the Crown ne'er requited.
Loss of Estate, Relations, Blood,
Was too well known, but did no good.
With long Campaigns & paines oth'
Gout,
He could no longer hold it out.
Always a restless life he led,
Never at quiet till quite dead.
He marry'd in his latter dayes,
One who exceeds the comon praise,
But wanting breath still to make known
Her true Affection and his Own,
Death kindly came, all wants supply'd
By giving Rest, which life deny'd."

It must not be omitted, however, that the pewing of St. Michael's Church is altogether a gross incongruity; but it is satisfactory to know that the means have been secured for getting rid of this defect, and that a determination has been come to by the vestry for entirely new-pewing the Church, for which purpose Mr. Richard Burgh, a native of Coventry, left by will, in 1803, the sum of £1,000. This legacy was not paid till 1817, since which time, subject to some abatements, the interest thereon has been accumulating, and, together with the principal, now amounts to almost, if not quite enough, to defray the cost of carrying into effect this important object, " in a proper and decent manner, and becoming the dignity thereof," as enjoined by the testator.

St. Michael's Church is renowned for possessing one of the finest peals of bells in England, ten in number, which in 1794 were re-hung upon a stupendous and most ingenious wooden framework within the tower, rising from the ground, and altogether unconnected with the walls, in order to avoid damage or danger thereto.

The vestry of the Church, in shape and dimensions not very unlike a ship's cabin, has some very antique oak furnishings, together with a good portrait painting of the late Rev. Robert Simson, who died on May 16th, 1846, having held the vicarage for upwards of 52 years.

There are a number of Charities belonging to this Church, chiefly consisting of sums bequeathed for distributing bread, bibles, and clothing to the poor.

The living is in the gift of the Crown, and the *net* value was returned by the Ecclesiastical Commissioners in 1831 at £472 per annum.

TRINITY CHURCH.

Dugdale gives no certain clue for determining the period at which this Church was founded. "Of this," says he, "the first mention I find is, of its appropriation to the Priory in 44 Henry 3rd (that is to say, in the year 1260). In 1291 it was valued at 20 marks, and the vicarage at 2 marks. But in 26th Henry 8th the said vicarage was valued at £33. Is. 6d."

The close proximity of this edifice to St. Michael's, is highly disadvantageous to it in a comparison of the two—a misfortune which has been still further heightened by the bad taste and anomalous features exhibited in the manner in which the outer repairs of it have been done at various times during the last half century; for although the recent restoration of the west front is executed in a far better style, there are still such glaring errors, and so much evidence of incompleteness meeting the eye at every other point, that little can be said in praise of the exterior. The north side being greatly dilapidated, a determination was come to by the vestry a few months ago to effect its renovation in an appropriate and substantial manner; and at the time these pages go to press, the work is in progress.

The building approximates to the form of a cross, which for exclusively religious edifices was a favourite form in early times. A square tower rises from the centre, and is continued by a good spire. The original spire, however, was blown down in 1664, upon the body of the Church, which thereby sustained considerable damage. In three years afterwards the new spire was completed, and the roof of the Church restored. The tower is 99 feet, the spire 132 feet, and the spindle of the weathercock 6 feet; the entire height from the ground to the summit being 237 feet.

The Church comprises chancel and nave, and north and south aisles. The four pillars and

K arches in the centre, which support the tower, are massive, but well-proportioned. The pulpit, a very ancient one, is of stone, and accounted to be one of the finest in the kingdom, as is also the font of this Church.

In the year 1831, in the course of cleaning the Church, a very extraordinary fresco painting was discovered in the space above the springing of the west arch under the tower, and extending to the roof of the Church. The accumulations of dirt and old whitewash having been removed from the surface, the picture was found to exhibit a curious representation of the Last Judgment. In the centre is our Saviour clothed in a crimson robe, seated, as would appear, on a rainbow, with the earth as his footstool. Below are the Virgin Mary and St. John the Baptist, and the twelve Apostles, arranged six on each side. Two angels are sounding the summons to judgment, and the tombs are giving up their dead. On the right of our Saviour is shown a flight of steps leading to a portico, over which angels are looking down on the dread scene; while others are engaged in giving welcome reception to the figure of a man wearing a tiara, and evidently intended to represent a Pope, who, having passed St. Peter, may be supposed the first permitted to enter Heaven. On the left hand of the Judge are the unhappy spirits condemned to exclusion

from the abodes of bliss, and who, in the most unaccountable attitudes, are being removed by devils into the place of torment. As a relic, it is interesting from its antiquity; but is otherwise less attractive.

There are but few monuments in Trinity Church; and perhaps the tablet possessing most interest is that to Dr. Philemon Holland, on the south wall of the choir, who resided in this city, and exercised the double profession of schoolmaster and physician. He was a great translator from the classic languages; and it is said that he prided himself in having written a folio volume with one pen,—an old one when he commenced, and not quite worn out when the volume was concluded.

In 1833, during the time that the Rev. W. F. Hook (now Dr. Hook) held the vicarage, some extensive alterations were made at the east end of the Church in the improvement of the Altar-piece, and beautifying and adorning of the Communion-table, which is a fine piece of antique oak carved work, in excellent preservation. At the same time the window over the altar was filled up with stained glass, exhibiting various religious emblems, the Royal arms, and other heraldry. In the Vestry of the Church is a good half-length portrait of Dr. Hook.

There formerly existed a building called "Jesus Hall," adjoining the south transept of this Church, and underneath was an arched passage and public road. This archway, however, was stopped and enclosed in the year 1834, and converted into a sort of lumber-room; at the same time, also, the old footways through the Churchyard were diverted to the outside of it; and it was partly enclosed by a fence of iron palisades,—alterations which certainly have contributed much to that quiet which is most seemly in a resting-place for the dead.

Trinity Church is rich in estates bequeathed for its benefit, and which at the present time yield nearly £1,000 annually. This excellent resource is the means of saving the parishioners from the imposition of a church-rate. There are also numerous charities left to be

disposed of by the Churchwardens and Overseers, in various modes for the relief the poor.

The living is in the gift of the Crown, and the net annual value in 1831 was returned at £396. The present Vicar is the Rev. John Howells.

8ALNT JOHN'S CHURCH.

Isabel, the Queen-mother of Edward III. , assigned the land of this site (117 feet in length and 40 feet in breadth), at that time called ' Babbelake," for the building of a Chapel in honour of our Saviour and St. John the Baptist, and which was finished in five years, and dedicated on the 6th of May, 1350. In a survey taken in 1534, it was called " The College of Babbelake;" and in 1545 its revenues were found to be £111. 13s. 8d. per annum. Adjoining to this Chapel there was anciently a residence for the seclusion of an Anchorite.

On being made a Rectory and a Parish Church by Act of Parliament in 1734, it was repaired and pewed, and the living settled on the Head Master of the Free School. The patronage was vested in the Corporation, and continued so till the passing of the Municipal Corporations Act of 1834, after which it was assigned to the local Trustees of the Church Charities.

The building, which is cruciform, must, in its original state, have been a very handsome one, with a neat, though not very lofty tower rising in the centre; but the outside of the Church, especially the tower, is now in a very dilapidated state, and even in its repairs in former times, has been shockingly defaced in some of its best parts. In 1841, however, the beautiful west window was restored in its original character; and during the year 1846 the stone-work of the same window was renewed in corresponding good taste.

The interior of the Church, which has a noble appearance, is in a far better state of repair, though there are here many marks of mutilation of the fine original architecture. It consists of nave, transepts, chancel, and aisles; and near to the western window stands a finely-executed font, erected in 1843. There is a good organ, which was built in 1817, and placed across the chancel; but in 1845 it was removed from this situation, and set up on the north side of the chancel, under the superintendence of Mr. W. Chater, the organist, by whom it was also at the same time repaired and improved in its movements.

There are a few charitable bequests belonging to this Church, for distribution in bread and clothing to the poor, and for the performance of certain extra services.

The net annual value of the living was returned in 1831 at £83. This, however, is independent of the emolument derived from the Head Mastership of the Free School before described.

St. John's Church is situate at the extremity of the lower end of Spon-street; and in this street a Wake is held on the Sunday, and two following days, after St. John's day. These institutions were anciently feasts on the dedication of Churches; but the custom soon degenerated, as appears by the following quotation from an old manuscript legend of St. John the Baptist, given by Dugdale:—

' And ye shall understond and know how the *Evyns* were furst found in old time. In the beginning of holi Chirche, it was so that the pepull cam to the Chirche with candellys brennyng, and wold *Wake* and come with light toward night to the Chirche in their devocions; and aftir they fell to lecherie, and songs, daunses, harping, piping, and also to glotony and sinne, and so tourned the holinesse to cursydness; wherefore, holi faders ordeined the pepull to leve that *Waking,* and to fast the *Evyn.* But it is called *Vigilia,* that is *Waking* in English; and it is callyd the Evyn, for at Evyn they were wont to come to Chirche."

CHRIST CHURCH.

This is a pleasing and well-built modem edifice, attached to the parish Church of St. Michael, erected on the scite of the Grey Friars' Monastery, the spire of which was given by the Corporation of Coventry about twenty years ago, and now forms an important and conspicuous portion of the present structure; which was consecrated and opened for public worship on the 3rd of August, 1832. The style of the principal entrance or south-west front, is considerably decorated, consisting of a large centre finely arched doorway, with smaller ones on each side, having windows over them, and the whole surmounted by pinnacles and a cross. The inside of the Church is distinguished by elegant simplicity. The nave is 101 feet in length with side aisles. It is galleried, and is calculated to accommodate 1500 persons, of whom upwards of 900 are enjoined to be free sittings. The small and inadequate organ, which formerly stood in the western gallery, has lately been replaced by a new one, built by Banfield of Birmingham, possessing a fine tone, and in all respects an admirable instrument.

ST. PETER'S CHURCH.

St. Peter's Church, Hill Field, Harnall, or New Town, as it is sometimes called, originally bore the same relationship to the Parish Church of the Holy Trinity as Christ Church does to St. Michael's; but in 1842 it was made a district church. St. Peter's Church, however, is a fragile, tasteless building of brick and mortar, presenting no feature of particular interest. It was erected in 1840-1, on a piece of land given by Mr. Charles Weston, of Canley, by whom the first stone was laid; and it was opened on the 28th of October, 1841, to meet the religious wants of the increasing population of the district in which it stands. The building is 131 feet 6 inches long, and 56 feet 8 inches wide; and it furnishes 559 appropriated sittings, and 695 free.

There is a pleasing cemetery adjoining the Church, and since its erection a commodious school room has been built in the immediate vicinity, on a plot of ground given for the purpose by Joseph Gilbert, Esq.

DISTRICT OF ST. THOMAS. In the year 1844 a portion of St. John's parish was set apart by ecclesiastical authority, L under the name of St. Thomas's District, and assigned to the spiritual superintendence of a separate Clergyman appointed thereto. The district comprises the whole of Spon-End beyond the bridge, and all that part of the parish from thence, lying south-west of the river Sherbourn. The Corporation of Coventry, in furtherance of the objects contemplated in this arrangement, gave up, so far as their interests were concerned as Lords of the Manor, a piece of common land by the side of Summerland Butts, consisting of one acre and twenty-eight perches, as a site for the erection of a church to the new district. A sum of £81 was paid as compensation for the interest of the freemen of this City in the land in question; and though some opposition was made by a portion of that body against the alleged violation of their rights by this appropriation, the grant of land was sanctioned and confirmed, and in a short time hence the object will, in all probability, be carried into effect. The services for this district have in the interim been conducted at the Thomas-Street Infant School, the use of which is liberally granted by Mr. Cash, a member of the Society of Friends, whose property it is.

PLACES OP WORSHIP *Belonging to the different Denominations of Dissenters.*

In enumerating the places of worship in Coventry belonging to the several denominations of Dissenters, the oldest is THE GREAT MEETING, In Smithford-street, erected in 1701. A congregation of Dissenters bad previously assembled in an old building in West-orchard, called "Leather Hall," which at one time had been used by certain ejected clergy of the Established Church. It is a large old-fashioned chapel, fitted up with oak pews and galleries, and is in comparatively good repair. It has been for many years occupied by the Unitarians. There is a charity called "Smith's Charity," yielding about.£100 a-year, at the disposal of the trustees of this meeting-house.

VICAR-LANE CHAPEL. The original chapel of this name was built in 1723, by John Moore, an alderman of Coventry, who also endowed it with some amount of property. The first minister of this place of worship was the Rev. Robert Simson, M.A., grandfather of the late Vicar of St. Michael's Church. In 1822 the chapel was new-fronted and much enlarged, and will now accommodate upwards of 1200 persons. It has always been devoted to the services of the Independents. WEST-ORCHARD CHAPEL. This is another Independent Chapel, the original having been erected in 1777, and enlarged at several subsequent periods. In 1820 it was taken down, the site in front cleared by the removal of some old tenements, and the present commodious place of worship was built. Including the school gallery, it will accommodate about 1500 persons.

THE FRIENDS' MEETING-HOUSE,

Situate in Vicar-lane, is a building the exact date of the erection of which is involved in some obscurity. It is known, however, that the people called Quakers are of very long standing in Coventry, for the celebrated William Penn is said to have had an interview with them at their "meeting-house *in Hill-street,*" (probably in a building on the site of their present burying ground there,) so early as the year 1687. Their present chapel is believed to have been built or completed about the middle of the last century.

COW-LANE CHAPEL *(Particular Baptists J.*

This is a very neat place of worship, and was erected in the year 1793, though there had previously existed a small Baptist Chapel in Jordan-well. The present chapel, which is within an enclosed yard, will accommodate upwards of 800 persons.

WESLEY CHAPEL.

The Wesleyans have occupied several places of worship in succession in Coventry. The little chapel once belonging to the Baptists, up a court in Jordan-well, (now converted into two tenements there,) was, for some time, used by this body, who afterwards removed to a chapel near Gosford-bridge, built in 1808 for a congregation of Independents, which in a few years was dissolved. The Gosford-street Chapel, however, being an extremely frail building, was taken down after a brief existence of little more than 20 years; and the Wesleyans, by exertion, raised their present structure, situate in Warwick-lane, and opened it for worship in the year 1836. It will hold about 900 persons.

SPON-END CHAPEL Was originally built as an Infant School in 1824. It is private property, and has been rented in turn by several denominations of Dissenters belonging to the larger chapels, to hold worship in, as they might see fit. WHITE-FRIARS' LANE CHAPEL Was completed in 1825, for the General Baptists, for whom it provides about 450 sittings. WELL-STREET CHAPEL *(Independents,)* Is, in the interior, an agreeable-looking and well-built place of worship. It was erected in 1827, and provides seats for 700 persons. GROVE-STREET CHAPEL. This is a small place of worship, affording accommodation to about 300 persons, and was erected in Grove-street, on the east side of Milllane, by the Primitive Methodists, in 1836.

There is good school-room accommodation adjoining most of the above chapels.

HILL-FIELD CHAPEL And School Room is in connexion with the West-orchard Chapel congregation, by whose efforts it was raised, in 1836, for the accommodation of that populous district. THE ROMAN CATHOLIC CHURCH.

A Roman Catholic Chapel was erected at the top of Hill-street, in this City, in the year 1807. Its inadequacy for the requirements of the community to whose religious services it was devoted, together with the inroads of decay, rendered its demolition necessary a few years ago, and on the 29th of May, 1843 (the Rev. Dr. Ullathorne then holding the priesthood), the first stone was laid of the present modern gothic structure, which, for durability of materials, excellency of workmanship, and appropriateness of design, supplies conclusive evidence that the Roman Catholics of the present day are by no means behindhand of their forefathers in the art and true conception of church-building. This church stands immediately adjoining the site of the old chapel, in a commanding point of view, and was dedicated under the name of "The Church of the most Holy Sacrament." It consists of nave, with clerestory, north and south aisles, chancel, lady chapel, and sacristies. There is a tower at the southwest corner of the church, intended to

be at some future day surmounted by a spire, rising, according to the design, to the height of 130 feet from the ground. The entire length of the church inside is 115 feet, its breadth 50 feet. The whole of the interior finishing is highly beautiful, rich in ornament, and abounding in the impressive symbols belonging to the Roman Catholic faith. The Ladye Chapel is a perfect gem of the kind. There is an excellent organ, built by Messrs. Bevington, of London, which stands in a small gallery at the northwest corner. The services are performed by members of the order of St. Benedict; and adjoining the church is a house or presbytery, constructed on the principle of a Benedictine Priory.

ENDOWED SCHOOLS.

Besides the Free School, which has already been noticed under the head of "St. John's Hospital and Free School," Coventry has a number of other endowed schools, viz.:— BABLAKE SCHOOL,

Founded in 1560, by Mr. Thomas Wheatley, Mayor of Coventry, and held in eligible buildings in the immediate vicinity of Bond's Hospital. The revenues now amount to upwards of £900 a year, and furnish the means for a good BAKER, BILLING, AND CROW'S SCHOOL. 91 plain education to about 50 boys, children of the working classes in Coventry, who are admitted when near eleven years of age, and continue two years, or till the usual period of apprenticeship. They are supplied with the principal articles of clothing immediately on admission, and at the end of the first year are taken into the house and wholly provided for, every attention being paid to secure them personal domestic comfort and salutary moral training. On their leaving the school they are apprenticed for seven years to such trades as may be chosen for them by their parents or guardians.

This school, which was formerly under the control of the Corporation, is now under the management of the General Charity Trustees of Coventry. BAKER, BILLING, AND CROW'S SCHOOL. This School, which is situate in Cowlane, was founded by Mr. Samuel Baker, of London, in the year 1690. The Charity was further augmented, by various benefactors, and its funds now realize nearly £500 a year. The property of the Charity is vested in seven trustees, most of whom are of the Unitarian persuasion, at the chapel belonging to which the boys regularly

M r attend public worship every Sunday. The Scholars, of whom there are about 50, are admitted from ten to eleven years of age, and remain in the school till they are nearly fourteen, during which time they are taught reading, writing, and arithmetic, and the elements of geography. Each boy has a suit of clothes, including cap, shoes, and stockings, annually; and when bound apprentice, a few pounds premium is also given.

THE BLUE COAT GIRLS' SCHOOL.

This School was established about the commencement of the last century by voluntary contributions; but its funds have increased since then, by gifts and bequests at various times, to the amount of upwards of £1,500. The Charity is managed by trustees, consisting of the Vicar and Vestrymen of Trinity Parish, whose annual income from the School estates is about.£135, which income is augmented by the proceeds of a charity sermon, preached at Trinity Church every year, yielding usually rather more than £100. Forty girls, children of the labouring classes, are taught and partly clothed out of the funds of this Charity. They are admitted at ten years of age, and stay from three to five years, daring which period they are taught to read, knit, and sew. The six oldest girls are taken into the House the last year, and instructed by the Mistress in such duties as may fit tbem for becoming useful domestic servants. The School stands on the site, and is connected with the remains, of the west end of the Cathedral in Priory-row.

BAYLBY'S CHARITY SCHOOL,

Founded by the will of Mrs. Katherine Bayley, in the year 1723, provides a good plain education for about 40 boys, who are admitted at eleven years of age, and remain in the School till they are fourteen, when they are apprenticed

with a premium of £3. They receive also a suit of clothes annually while in the School, and attend regularly at St. Michael's Church, of which parish the Founder was an inhabitant.

From time to time various legacies and donations have been given in augmentation of this Charity, the income of which, from real and funded property, now amounts to nearly £160 a year, besides the proceeds of a charity sermon annually at St. Michael's Church. About two years ago a new and substantial School, with the requisite furnishings, was erected down a 94 QUAKERS' SCHOOL—FAIRFAX'S SCHOOL.

yard in Little Park-street, on land belonging to the estate. The expenditure on account of maintaining the School is about,£200 a year. SOUTHERN AND CEANER'S CHARITY SCHOOL.

This School, now held in Vicar-lane, was founded in the years 1729 and 1731, by the wills of Bridget Southern and Frances Craner, both members of the Society of Friends, for the " education or bringing up of poor children of the people called 'Quakers,' or others, being inhabitants of Coventry."

The property is vested in trustees, and yields nearly £90 a year; but as there are no children in Coventry belonging to the Society of Friends requiring gratuitous instruction, others, to the number of between 30 and 40, are chosen at the discretion of the trustees. They are admitted at eight years of age, and continue in the School three years, during which term they are partly clothed, and taught reading, writing, and plain needlework.

FAIRFAX'S CHARITY SCHOOL.

This School originated in a donation of £100, made by Mr. Samuel Fairfax, in the year 1751; but subsequent benefactions have raised its income to about £200 a year, besides the receipt of a charity sermon collection of at least £100, at St. Michael's Church. From these resources forty boys of the industrious poor are clothed and educated for a term of three years previous to being bound apprentice. The School is in Sponstreet, and its affairs are managed by eight trustees resident in St. John's

Parish.

Besides the above enumerated Endowed Schools there are several other schools, which are supported chiefly by voluntary contributions. The principal of these are the following:— THE BRITISH SCHOOL

Was founded in 1811, on the system and under the direction of the celebrated Joseph Lancaster. For many years it was held in a large and cheerless building down a yard near St. John's Bridge, commonly known as the Riding School Yard, from the building having been formerly used as a circus. In the year 1840, however, an effort was made by the friends of the institution, and a new school was erected in King-street, and which since that time has been much improved in its internal conveniences, and is now a very commodious one.

THE NATIONAL SCHOOLS

For boys and girls, situate in Union-street, and in immediate proximity to Christ Church, were erected in 1826, at a cost of above.£1,500. They are built in the Elizabethan style, with a dwelling-house in the centre, and two wings forming the school rooms are raised upon groined arches, underneath which are the playgrounds for the children. These schools are supported entirely by the Clergy and members of the Church of England.

ST. JOHN'S DAY AND SUNDAY SCHOOLS.

The erection of these schools, which took place in 1839, in the Holyhead Road, Sponstreet, is mainly attributable to the liberality of Richard Kevitt Rotherham, Esq., formerly Mayor of this City, and now one of the Justices of the Peace, he having given the land as a site, and contributed.£100 towards the building, which, besides the school rooms, comprises a dwelling-house for master and mistress. THE ROMAN CATHOLIC SCHOOLS Are in the immediate vicinity of their church, in Hill-street. There are also several INFANT SCHOOLS in different parts of the City, all of which are well attended. THE SCHOOL OF DESIGN. The establishment of a School of Design in Coventry, which took place in 1843, arose entirely from the strong sense entertained by many of the principal inhabitants, that to a City like this, whose interests are so closely interwoven with the prosperity of the silk manufacture, such an institution was of paramount necessity, as a means of cultivating the taste of the youthful part of our artizan population, and instructing them in the art of design, in the hope that in due time its advantage would be felt in that intense rivalry which has so long prevailed between the British and the French manufacturer. The school is aided by grants from the Government, and its rules and general management are subject to the supervision and inspection of the Government School at Somerset House. THE MECHANICS' INSTITUTION. This institution has arisen from a small beginning in 1828, and from then during a 98 RELialOCS KNOWLEDGE SOCIETY—LIBRARY. number of years struggled on under many difficulties; but by the perseverance of a few firm friends it has gradually succeeded, and now forms an establishment of some importance and value. It is held in Hertford-street, in a building purchased and fitted up for the purpose, and which now comprises a theatre, reading room, class rooms, and library. It is governed by a committee, chosen annually by the members. RELIGIOUS AND USEFUL KNOWLEDGE SOCIETY.

This Society was formed in 1835, chiefly by the exertions of the Rev. Dr. Hook, who was at that time Vicar of Trinity Parish, in this City. Its objects are, in some respects, similar to those of the Mechanics' Institution; but it enjoins with greater strictness a regard to religious teaching in the books forming its library. Indeed, it is avowedly conducted on the principles of the Church of England. Its rooms are in Little Park-street.

COVENTRY SUBSCRIPTION LIBRARY Was formed in 1791, and was originally kept at the north end of the old Broad Gate. It is now held in Hertford-street, in a building which was first erected as a place of worship by a small sect of persons who attempted to set up an amalgamation of Church of Englandism and Dissent in their forms of public service; but which soon dwindled away, and the building was bought by the Library Society. The library is a very voluminous one, but the subscribers do not exceed two hundred members. The rate of subscription is from one to two guineas, according to the privileges of which parties choose to avail themselves, there being a commodious news and reading room connected with the institution.

THE BARRACKS.
In the year 1793 the site of the once famous "Bull Inn," the spot upon which Henry 7th had been greeted with civic feasting; and where the hapless Mary Queen of Scots was once incarcerated as a prisoner;—this site, memorable for the diversity of scenes and events associated therewith, was appropriated to the erection of the present Barracks, which are calf pable of affording good quarters to two troops-of cavalry, and are in all respects held to be conveniently and healthily situated. The front is built of stone, and is entered from Smithford Street, through an arched gateway, above which are the royal arms. In this part of the building are the most commodious apartments, which are of course assigned for the accommodation of the superior officers. Passing from thence, through a long avenue of stables, a fine spacious yard opens to the view, connected immediately with the green fields. Around the yard are the usual offices and buildings connected with a military establishment, comprising storehouses, guardroom, riding-school, hospital, &c. The outer or back gate opens from the " Bull Yard" to the Warwick road.

THE POST OFFICE. For a long series of years Coventry has had to suffer the inconvenience and disgrace of one of the most miserable substitutes for a Post Office that ever existed. The fact, that up to the moment when this paragraph is written, a rapidly increasing population, now numbering for the City alone at least thirty-four thousand souls, and with a thickly inhabited district of eight or ten hamlets and villages, all in a very great measure identical with Coventry in manufacturing and trading pursuits;—the fact that the Post Office transactions of so large a population have up to this time been conducted in one little room about fourteen feet square, with only a small pitch-hole, the size of an ordinary pane of glass, in front, for the convenience of the public, exposed to the weather at all seasons, and sometimes actually blocking up the footpath, in consequence of the delays to which they have had necessarily to submit;—that such a Post Office has existed up to this time, will scarcely be believed. It is, however, satisfactory to be enabled to state that probably by the time these pages come before the public, this monstrous inconvenience will be got rid of. In the year 1846 a memorial to the Post Office authorities in London was presented by a deputation, comprising members of the Town Council and some of the principal manufacturers of Coventry, representing this grievance. After overcoming some minor impediments and objections as to the situation of another office, and the degree of aid which the General Post Office department would afford towards facilitating the improvement, the Town Council made terms for the lease of the large and commodious house in Smithford-street, opposite the Barracks, which has undergone the requisite alterations and fittings up for the purpose. This place, although of course it does not outwardly exhibit all the grace of appearance which a newly-erected Post Office would possess, is nevertheless roomy and convenient, and has the advantage of being in such close vicinity to the old office as to be at once distinguishable, as also from its being opposite the Barracks. There are two arrivals and departures of London letters, and those of Manchester, Liverpool, and the north generally, every day. The Post Office-box here closes at ten o'clock every night, but letters may be posted as late as a quarter past eleven, on payment of a penny extra. Morning letters for London must be posted here before nine o'clock a.m., and for the reception of Liverpool, Manchester, and the north of England letters, the box closes at ten minutes before twelve o'clock in the day. In both cases, however, letters are taken in nearly an hour later, on payment of the extra penny.

Besides the chief office in Smithford Street, it has been resolved to establish two Branch Offices, or Receiving Houses; viz. one in Jordan Well and another in the neighbourhood of Bishop Street: but all letters delivered at these Receiving Houses must be either stamped or left unpaid, as no money will be taken there.

A part of the premises taken under the above-named lease, are relet by the Corporation as offices for the Excise Department of this District, but totally distinct from the Post Office.

THE THEATRE.

In close proximity to the Post Office and the Barracks, but secluded from public view up a yard on the south side of Smithford Street, stands the Theatre. It was erected by the late Sir Skears Rew, a member of the Corporation of Coventry, and opened for public performances on Easter Monday, 1819. As a provincial theatre it is tastefully fitted up, and will accommodate about fifteen hundred persons. The lease of it has been held for many years by Mr. Henry Bennett, under whose superintendence it usually opens about Christmas, and continues to offer a succession of entertainments for three or four months.

THE GAS WORKS. These works, which are situated in Naul's Mill Lane, at the extremity of the inhabited part of the town, on the north-west side, were erected in the year 1821, as a speculation by a number of private gentlemen. Before the works were completed, however, an Act of Parliament was obtained, under which a company was formed, having 800 shares of £25, and the whole concern was bought for £20,000. In the hands of this company the management of the works continued till about three years ago, when Mr. A. Angus Croll took them on a lease for ten years. In his hands the mains have been considerably extended, and under engagements with the Town Council, the old oil lamps have been, in the same proportion, superseded. The mains in the principal streets have also been re-

placed by pipes of larger calibre; but still it must be admitted that the present requirements of the town for its supply of gas have far outgrown the calculations on which these works were at first undertaken. The present price of gas from them, is 9s. per 1,000 feet to consumers.of under 5,000 feet, but lower in proportion to the larger amount consumed; the average price being 7s. 6d. per thousand feet. A discount of 5 per cent, is returned for prompt payment.

THE WATERWORKS. Under the covenants of a two hundred years lease, which expired last year, Coventry has been provided with its antiquated waterworks at Swanswell from time immemorial. To say that the supply of water which such materials could yield, has long been totally incommensurate with the town's wants, is superfluous, except as a preliminary remark to noticing the new works which were commenced in the early part of last year, and which are now approaching to their completion. The site of these works is at Sponend, in a field just by the side of the brook, a spot where a confluence of prolific springs of good water presented signal advantages for such a purpose. The erection of them has been done according to a plan prepared by Mr. Hawkesley, an eminent engineer; and although some difficulties were met with in making the excavations for the filtering bed, arising from the great influx of water, such difficulties were successfully grappled with, and the work constructed in a most complete and substantial manner, and upon soundly scientific principles. The engine, as per contract, is of the kind usually known as the Boulton and Watt rotation condensing engine, and is of forty-horse power. The diameter of the different pipes for distributing the water through the town varies from seven to fourteen inches; the entire length of the mains being from twelve to thirteen miles. There is an ample reservoir formed on an elevated piece of land near the top of Bishop-street, formerly the Bowling Green, and a field adjoining, which is capable of containing nearly a million gallons of water, the situation of which, in a

straight line, is nearly half a mile distant from the works. It is calculated that the supply of water obtained from the various sources at Spon-end, will be 700,000 gallons per day, or considerably more than double the yield of both the old works in the Conduit Meadow and at Swanswell. The probable amount of the entire outlay will be about £20,000. THE CEMETERY.

This truly great and important undertaking was commenced almost simultaneously with that of the waterworks, and has been forwarded at about the same rate of progress. A situation more appropriate—a spot of ground more serenely picturesque, could not have been selected, or even desired, than that fixed upon for this interesting object. It consists of a piece of land comprising nearly eighteen acres, lying by the right hand side of the old London turnpike road, and is bounded at the southern end by the wall of the London and Northwestern Railway: thus reaching in this direction to the extreme limits of the City. On the other side, it is surrounded by the narrow green lanes leading to the Park gardens and Whitley Common. The ground itself, before any operations were begun, presented throughout a beautiful alternation of mound and hollow, covered with rich herbage, and skirted completely by rows of tall elms, and which still form the fine natural ornament of its borders, which however have been further fenced by a stone wall. The laying out of the Cemetery has been executed from a plan made by Mr. Paxton, head gardener to his Grace the Duke of Devonshire; and the work itself superintended by Mr. Ashwell, another agent, we believe, on the noble domain of Chatsworth, whose united skill and perfect taste have already produced one of the most delightful scenes of the kind in the whole kingdom, alike creditable to the public spirit of this ancient city, as it must be promotive of the public health of the town, by putting an end to the excessive deposit of o human remains in the too long over-crowded burying grounds which exist in the very midst of a dense population.

The Cemetery is entered at the north

end, through a commodious gateway, adjoining which is the keeper's lodge, a simple stone structure with a kind of tower=summit to correspond with the other side of the entrance. The ground is mainly divided eastward and westward, by a capacious serpentine walk, but without in the least diminishing the harmonious effect of the whole. In settling the question as to the appropriation of the different parts, it was determined by lot, at a meeting of the Town Council, that the west side be assigned to the use of the members of the Church of England, and the east side to the several denominations of Dissenters, including the Roman Catholic. Towards the near end of the Church of England compartment, stands the chapel for the performance of the burial service, a substantial stone edifice in the Norman style, and in all respects suited to its object. The chapel for the funeral services of the other religious communities, is also of stone, and from a design after the Italian style of architecture, and stands near the farther end of their division. With ample space allotted for the purposes of interment, the ground is intersected throughout by gravel walks bordered by shrubs, flowers, and evergreens, and interspersed with ornamental saplings, which meet the eye with luxuriant variety in every direction.

The still unfinished state of the work must necessarily render the present description imperfect; but enough of it is already executed to warrant the recommendation to all visitors of a walk to this delightful scene, the beauty and perfect order of which, it may be hoped, will always be preserved from molestation by rude hands, while the serious nature of its primary use should secure from all the respect of a becoming demeanour while surveying its attractions.

The outlay for the Cemetery will be about J12.000.

It is here proper to state that by the Acts of Parliament, under the provisions of which the Cemetery and Waterworks have been formed, the Corporation are empowered to make other improvements, and have already purchased the properties preparatory to abating the nuisances of the two Mill-dams.

THE RAILWAY STATION. The London and Birmingham Railway (the Company of which, having extended its undertakings, is now called the " London and North Western"), was opened for the public on the 9th of April, 1838. This Company, from some unaccountable cause, has from first to last underrated the amount of Coventry traffic. Its first Station, situated a few hundred yards from the town, close to the bridge on the Warwick-road, still stands, a remarkable evidence of the folly of whoever might have planned it; resembling as it does a quiet little villa residence for an old maid or bachelor, rather than a railway station in the very centre of England, and erected for a town of between 30,000 and 40,000 souls, comprehending various busy hives of industry, whose products or supplies required constant interchange of conveyance to and from London, as well as the North of England. The gross error committed in the first instance soon forced upon the Company the necessity of applying a corrective, and a Station more adequate to the public requirements was built, about 100 yards distant from the first, and the approach to which is by a gentle descent down a good open road made for the purpose.

During several years no provision whatever was made for the Coventry luggage trade, and the inconvenience which manufacturers and tradespeople experienced from having to follow London parcels to the Birmingham Station, in order to get possession of them, produced many complaints and remonstrances, which finally led to the erection of a luggage station here. This luggage station, however, is a most unsightly, and, in some respects, a dangerous affair for those whose business brings them to it. It is built upon the south bank, on the right hand side of the Railway-bridge, the passenger station being in the other direction. The Company has a Branch Line to Leamington, and has obtained powers for making other lines, and enlarging their stations, in this locality. An enclosed and covered bridge over the line, and immediately adjoining the Station, has just been completed exclusively for the purpose of passengers, to obviate the danger of crossing the rails on the arrival or departure of trains.

THE CANAL.

The Coventry Canal commences at the top of Bishop-street. Its length is rather more than 32 miles, terminating at Fradley Heath, and, through the medium of various other canals, it communicates with London, Liverpool, Manchester, &c. An immense trade with the coal districts of Warwickshire is still carried on by means of this Canal, the shares of which were at one time a most valuable investment, being as high as £1,350 for the £100 share. Their value, however, has been greatly diminished by the railway competition which has of late years grown up, and they are now quoted much lower.

The Canal Company's office stands opposite the top of Bishop-street, and in immediate connexion with the Wharf. The Act for making the Coventry Canal was obtained in 1768.

BANKS.

Of the Banking Establishments in Coventry, the oldest is that of *Messrs. Little and Woodcock,* situate in High-street, opposite Broad-gate. There is further, that of the *Coventry and Warwickshire Banking Company,* established in 1836, and since incorporated with the Bank of Messrs. Beck and Prime, on whose newly-erected premises in High-street it has ever since been held. In the same year the *Coventry Union Banking Company* was formed, with which the Bank of Messrs. Bunney and Pepper was soon afterwards united. It is situate at the corner of Little Park-street, High-street.

THE SAVINGS' BANK.

A Savings' Bank was established in Coventry in 1835, for which year its report states the amount of its deposits to be £1,411. 7s. 8d. An account published in May, 1847, reports the investments then in the Bank of England, from this Institution, at £66,881. 9s. 9d.; and the number of accounts open, 3,073.

The Savings' Bank, which is held in a compartment of the Coventry Library, in Hertfordstreet, is open for business on Mondays and Fridays, from 12 till 2 o'clock; and on Saturday evenings, from 6 o'clock till 8.

MEDICAL INSTITUTIONS. In the year 1831, a prominent topic of discussion amongst the wealthier classes of Coventry was that of establishing a Dispensary, in order to meet the wants of the poor in time of sickness; and as considerable difference of opinion prevailed as to the principle upon which it was most desirable such Institution should be founded, the result was the formation of two, respectively denominated " The Self-Supporting Dispensary," and "The General Dispensary." As these descriptions imply, the first relied for its maintenance on the small weekly contributions of the working classes who might avail themselves of its advantages, aided by the subscriptions and donations of honorary members. The General Dispensary, on the other hand, was based on the principle of benevolence or charity alone for the support of its funds. Both Dispensaries succeeded very well, and a few years ago the Self-Supporting, or as it is now called, "The Provident Dispensary," erected for itself premises at the bottom of St. Michael's Churchyard, where its business is now conducted. The following statement is copied from the annual report published in May last:—

"The total number of persons who have received medical aid from the Dispensary since its establishment in July, 1831, is 25,783.

Under treatment at last report 90
Attended during last year 2103
2193
Cured 2049
Relieved 43
Dead 27
Under treatment.. 74 2193"

The receipts and disbursements of the Provident Dispensary, under the several items of account, is about £500 a-year.

COVENTRY AND WARWICKSHIRE HOSPITAL.

The General Dispensary, founded on the principle of gratuitous assistance to the poor, having, as might be expected, in the midst of a dense manufacturing population, found the claims upon its benevolence to increase, turned its attention to a wider sphere of action for augmenting its resources, and thereby extending its usefulness, and by the perseverance of its original promoters at length succeeded far beyond the most sanguine expectations that could have been cherished. The plan of founding a Hospital, the advantages of which should be open to the County at large, was as warmly encouraged as the want of such an establishment in this neighbourhood in particular was universally admitted; and after a year or two of generous exertion, and an ineffectual attempt to unite the two Dispensaries for the purpose, this worthy object was carried into effect. A building of considerable extent with an enclosed garden, the whole occupying 1600 square yards of land, and in a healthy situation at the top of Little Parkstreet, close to the Coventry Park, was purchased and fitted up for the purpose; and for some years past the value of this important p 116 LYINQ-IN CHARITIES INDUSTRIAL HOME.

institution has been realized by thousands of objects in this City and in that part of the County of Warwick contiguous hereto, whom misfortune, poverty, or accident had placed in need of the assistance which it provides. There is accommodation for a considerable number of in-door patients, and its doors are always open for the reception and treatment of such as may by sudden and unforeseen casualties become the victims of physical suffering. The expenditure of the Hospital now is about.£1200 a-year, which is provided for entirely by the voluntary subscriptions and donations of its friends in this City and the adjacent parts of the County of Warwick. LYING-IN CHARITIES. There are two Lying-in Charities in Coventry, the purposes of which are sufficiently explained by the name they bear. They are both supported with a considerable degree of liberality. INDUSTRIAL HOME. In the year 1846, and chiefly by the exertions of a few ladies, an " Industrial Home" was established in Coventry. It consists of a goodsized dwelling house, eligibly situated near Swanswell Terrace, and is for the reception of young females who may have heen left so far neglected or unprovided for as to peril their future prospects in life, and render them objects deserving of protection. According to the first Report of the Institution, 25 girls had been admitted, of whom 14 were orphans, 4 had stepparents, one had been deserted by her mother and 3 by their fathers. They are religiously instructed, and trained to habits of industry, the proceeds of which are expended towards the maintenance of the establishment, which is otherwise supported by voluntary contributions. PROVIDENT INSTITUTION AND LOAN SOCIETY.

In the year 1841 was formed the "Provident Institution," which for small payments secures to the working classes all the legitimate advantages of benefit clubs, upon a far more economical principle. The plan of lending loans was also for some time adopted, but was eventually discontinued, being considered in some respects incompatible with its proper functions. A Loan Society was, however, established in a distinct form, and both Societies are now in a flourishing condition. The Provident Institution comprises 250 members. The Loan Society consists of 90 shareholders, who have a sum of £6000 lent out to about 2000 borrowers in sums varying from £1 to £15.

THE CHARITIES OP COVENTRY. The Charities belonging to the City of Coventry, intended for the benefit of the poor, are numerous and of large amount, and cannot now yield much less than £4000 annually, independently of those exclusively applied for educational purposes and hospitals for the aged. These Charities were formerly under the management of the Corporation, but by the operation of the Municipal Act of 1835 they are placed under the control of three separate sets of Trustees, respectively denominated, "The Church Charity Trustees," "The General Charity Trustees," and "The Trustees for Sir Thomas White's Estates." It must not, however, be inferred that the Church Charity Trustees exercise any authority over, or have any power of interference with the Charities of which the Churchwardens and parochial Overseers have the distribution. The Charities entrusted to the Church Charity Trustees are such of those of which the Corporation used to have the administration, in which the rights, the interests, or the principles of the church are supposed to be involved.

The most prominent and the largest benefactor to Coventry is the renowned Sir Thomas White, from the sources of whose liberality in the 16th century the "Four Pounds Charity" and the "City Fifties," or loan money, still flow. There are now about 210 of these "fourpounds" distributed every year in the month of October, to inhabitant householders, not being paupers. But an individual who has once received it is not eligible again within eleven years following. The loan money is for the purpose of lending out to freemen exclusively, in sums of £50, for a term of nine years, free of interest, but security satisfactory to the trustees, must be given, for repayment at the end of that period. In consequence of the inadequacy of the calls for these loans, there is a large accumulation of the fund, which now amounts to about £20,000. It has long been a subject of discussion amongst the freemen of Coventry, that it is desirable to obtain legislative sanction for the appropriation of at least a portion of this accumulated loan fund to some purpose more conducive to the benefit of the freemen at large; but in consequence of the divisions of opinion on the subject, as well with the trustees as the freemen, nothing yet has been done. Besides the above charities of Sir Thomas White, there are others annually given away at different periods to widows, freemen, and other needy persons. The principal of these are at Christmas and Ash Wednesday. At the firstnamed season, from 600 to 700 persons are presented with money in sums of 6s. 8d., 10s., 20s., and 30s. each; and at Ash Wednesday, from 500 to 600 persons are supplied in like manner. Many hundred tons of coal are also given away about these periods to individuals of the same class. A considerable

number of boys are also bound apprentice every year, with whom a premium of from £3 to £5 is given to the master (not being the parent), from charitable funds left for the purpose. A recent regulation of the trustees disqualifies any boy who cannot read and write, from being bound apprentice by them. The Trustees for these several Charities, as appointed by the Lord Chancellor in 1836, are as follows:— TRUSTEES OF SIR T. WHITE'S ESTATES.

Of the above Lists of Trustees, the following are now dead, viz.:—H. C. Adams, Charles Harris, Rev. R. Simson, Adie Cramp, Thomas Pepper, Samuel Vale, Joseph Soden, Joseph Howe, William Prime, Robert Bunney, and John Herbert.

The Rev. Dr. Hook, Rev. H. Maclean, James Beck, and James Wall, having gone to reside at a distance from Coventry, take no part in the affairs of the Charities.

THE LAMMAS LANDS. The Lammas Lands of Coventry are of very great antiquity, and there can be no doubt that at the time of their bestowal they were of immense benefit to the inhabitants. The Lammas and Michaelmas Lands are about 2,000 acres; the Commons about 300 acres. Custom and usage have for a long time past treated these lands as belonging, with a few exceptional cases, to the freemen of Coventry alone, of whom there are about 3,400. The Lammas right is that of turning on three head of cattle from the 13th of August, or in the case of the Michaelmas Lands, from Old Michaelmas-day, till Old Candlemasday. The Common right exists throughout the year. As this right of turning cattle on the Lammas is, at the present day, of practical use to only about a tenth part of the freemen, and gives rise to many abuses and much corruption in what is called the "fathering of cattle," many efforts have been made from time to time to get this right commuted into some other form more likely to render service to the entire body of freemen, as well as to emancipate the land itself from a condition prejudicial to its cultivation, and injurious to the City by presenting an obstacle to the progress of building. The disputes on this subject have given rise to fierce contentions and much bitterness, and have hitherto led to no really practical result, for although in the year 1845 the matter had proceeded so far as the bringing of a bill before Parliament for altering the Lammas right, or exchanging it for an equivalent, the object never reached a consummation, and it still appears as distant as ever. THE SENIORITY FUND. In the year 1843 an important step was taken by the freemen of

Coventry, assembled at a public meeting in St. Mary's Hall, for the purpose of adopting some mode of appropriating certain sums of money paid some years previously, and placed in the Bank of England, namely,—first, £105. 9s. 10d. , given by the Holyhead Road Commissioners in 1828; and second, £1,088, paid by the London and Birmingham Railway Company in 1834, as compensation for the rights of the freemen in portions of Lammas and Michaelmas land taken for these respective roads. These sums of money having accumulated largely by the interest arising therefrom, it was resolved, at the meeting above « referred to, to appoint four trustees for the freemen, to whom the money should be paid, and form a fund to be called *"The Freemen's Seniority Fund,"* the income arising from which fund should be paid, as far as the same might extend, in sums of 6s. per week, to the most aged freemen who should claim the same, according to their seniority upon the Corporation admission and enrolment book, such payment to be continued during their respective lives. This fund has since been augmented by monies arising in a similar manner from land required and taken for other public purposes, and it now affords a weekly allowance of the above-named amount to the *eight* senior freemen, some of whom have by this valuable resource been rescued from the workhouse. THE MAGISTRACY.

The police business of Coventry is administered by a Bench of Magistrates, who hold their sittings at the Mayoress's Parlour, St. Mary's Hall, every day except Tuesdays. The Court opens at 11 o'clock. The acting Magistrates are Thomas Banbury, Esq., who also fills the office of Mayor; T. Morris, Esq. , W. Hawkes, Esq., J. Ralphs, Esq., A. Herbert, Esq., J. Hands, Esq., R. K. Rotherham, Esq., T. Cope, Esq., R. Arrowsmith, Esq., M.D., and T. S. Morris, Esq. The County Magistrates hold a Petty Sessions on the second and fourth Thursdays in each month, in the Grand Jury Room of the County Hall.

THE CORPORATION. The municipal affairs of Coventry are managed by a Corporation or Town Council, constituted under the provisions of the Municipal Corporations Act. The members of the Council are returned from the five wards into which the town, *for this purpose,* is divided, viz.: Gosfordstreet Ward, White Friars Ward, Earl-street Ward, Spon-street Ward, and Bishop-street Ward, each ward having six representatives, two being elected by the burgesses annually, and consequently sitting for three years. There are also two Aldermen for each ward, who hold their seats in the Council for six years, and who are chosen by the Council, as is also the Mayor. The total number of burgesses, who are householders paying rates, is about 1,700. There is a stringent code of by-laws in existence, for the prevention of nuisances and annoyances, and the maintenance of orderly conduct in the public streets. A copy of these by-laws is constantly exhibited for public use in the gateway to St. Mary's Hall. The police force consists of chief constable, inspector, two Serjeants, and thirteen others. DIRECTORS OP THE POOR. By an Act of Parliament passed in the year 1801, the parishes of Coventry were united for the purposes connected with the management of the poor requiring relief. The business is confided to a Board of Directors consisting of 18 members, who sit for two years, nine being chosen annually on Easter Monday and Tuesday by the Guardians, whose qualification is that of being resident inhabitants, and rated at not less than £20 for the relief of the poor. The workhouse, (as stated in a former part of this work,) is erected on the site, and includes the remains, of the White Friars' Monastery, in an elevated and salubrious situation, near the top of Much Parkstreet. The management of this establishment is conducted in conformity with the regulations enjoined by the Poor Law Commissioners. THE TRADES OP COVENTRY. Although it is impossible to name the precise period when the textile art was first practised in Coventry; that its existence here in the weaving of tammies, camlets, shalloons, and other fabrics, chiefly of worsted, must be of great antiquity, is manifest from the names of those companies which are still familiar in our local annals; and in the year 1525, we find Henry Wall, *weaver,* filling the office of Mayor. The weaving of this description of goods, however, began to be superseded in the course of the last century, and for some years past has been wholly extinct. The ribbon trade was introduced here nearly a century and a half ago, by the grandfather of William Wilberforce Bird, who at one time represented this City in Parliament. In the list of Mayors of Coventry, we find the name of William Bird, *silkman,* for the year 1705. Mr. Bird is supposed to have been assisted, in the first establishment of his works, by the French refugees, who had been driven from their own country on account of their religious opinions. During a period of thirty or forty years after its introduction, the trade was confined to a very few hands, but afterwards began to spread itself into a wider sphere. The singlehand, or rather the single-shuttle, loom at first used, gradually gave way to the engine-loom, or many-shuttle loom; but this description of machinery consisted for a long time only of the old-fashioned Dutch loom, a specimen of which would now be something of a novelty.

Some important improvements in the art of figured ribbon weaving were made in Coventry, between 1818 and 1822, by several of our townsmen, manufacturers and operatives, a fact worthy of notice, because it goes to show that the spirit of progress was not entirely dormant prior to the application of the sharp spur of French competition, and the introduction of the Jacquard machine. But it is undoubtedly to these latter impulses that the high degree of perfection in which the ribbon trade of Coventry is now carried on is mainly attributable. Steam power is also brought in aid of this branch of trade in this City very extensively, there being six or eight factories worked by this agency, the principal of which are those of Messrs. J. and C. RatlifF in Hill-street, and of Messrs. Cope and Hammerton in King-street, each of these establishments giving employment to several hundred workpeople of both sexes. The total number of individuals engaged in the various departments of the ribbon trade of this City alone cannot be less than from 5,000 to 6,000. As auxiliaries to the silk trade, there are also several dyeing establishments, some of them of long standing, in Coventry, and where great excellence is evinced in the practice of this important chemical art. An extensive trade in the manufacture of fringes and gimp trimmings has also grown up within the last few years.

The other great sustaining branch of industry in Coventry is that of the Watch Trade. The manufacture of watches in this town has been carried on to some extent from a very remote period. George Porter, *watchmaker,* filled the office of Mayor in 1727. It has now become of such importance, that this is one of the principal marts both for the home and foreign trade. There are several very large factories; the largest is considered to be that connected with the firm of Messrs. R. K. Rotherbam and Sons, commonly spoken of as "The Old Factory." The factories of Messrs. Riley, and Messrs. Mercer, are also old establishments. Many others, doing a considerable business, have arisen in the last 25 years, within which period the amount of business done in Coventry has undoubtedly doubled.

It may be interesting to observe here, that amongst the papers comprised in the Harleian Library, and recorded in the Diary of Mr. Humphrey Wanley, a minute description is given of a most ingenious astronomical clock, made by a Mr. Watson, *of Coventry,* about the year 1689.

As every trade must in some measure ao commodate itself to the nature of the demand, so the ribbon and watch trades of Coventry, like all others, necessarily produce a considerable quantity of inferior goods—cheap imitations of excellence, to suit all sorts of customers. The taste and ability of Coventry manufacturers and artisans, however, is not to be tested by this standard; for in both cases it is undeniable that there are goods sent from our warehouses, which for intrinsic worth, and excellence of workman-

ship, are inferior to none in the United Kingdom.

THE BISHOPRIC OF COVENTRY.

The original Bishop's See of Lichfield was transferred to Chester in 1075, and thence removed to Coventry, in 1102, by Robert De Limesey, Bishop of Chester, who died and was buried in Coventry in 1117, after which time it was vacant four years. Robert Peche, Chaplain of King Henry I., was then consecrated thereto, under the title of "Bishop of Coventry and Lichfield." In 1188 the See was again re moved to Lichfield. Great contentions afterwards arose between the Chapters of Lichfield and Coventry as to the right or mode of election, but at length, in the reign of Henry the 3rd, the dispute was ended by an agreement that the Bishop should be elected both from Coventry and Lichfield, and that Coventry should take the precedence in the episcopal title: and thus it continued until the period of the restoration of Charles II., when, probably in consequence of the opposite parts taken by the two cities during the civil war, the precedency was given to Lichfield. In 1836 the Coventry portion of this diocese was, by the recommendation of the Ecclesiastical Commissioners, united with the See of Worcester, and the name of Coventry was no longer recognized in a bishop's title.

THE EARLDOM OP COVENTRY Originated with the descendants of John Coventry, of this City, who was Sheriff of London in 1416, and Lord Mayor in 1425. Thomas Coventry, a person of some eminence in the early part of the 17th century, and who held successively the offices of Solicitor-General in 1616, Attorney-General in 1620, and Lord Keeper of the Great Seal in 1625, was soon afterwards raised to the dignity of a Baron, by the title of Lord Coventry, of Aylesbury, in the County of Worcester. The Earls of Coventry have seldom been in any way connected with this City, either by property or residence.

FAIRS, RACES, &c.

Besides the Great Pleasure Fair already noticed, commencing on the Friday in Trinity week, and continuing eight days, there are also two other old annual

Cattle Fairs, one held on the 2nd of May, the other on the 2nd of November. There are also two Cheese Fairs, established a few years since by the Town Council, which are held in April and September, and monthly Cattle Fairs; but these latter have met with little support or custom hitherto. A Statute for the hiring of servants has been recently instituted, and is held about the first Tuesday after Old Michaelmas Day; but this Statute exists only by sufferance.

Although it is well known that the custom of annual *Races* in the Coventry Park prevailed at a remote date, such Races had for a long time sunk into total disuse, till about twelve years ago, when they were revived, first under the name of " Stoke Races," in consequence of the project of revival having been set on foot by several gentlemen residing in that parish, in which they also took place; but more ample support having been given to them, and from other reasons, they were subsequently denominated "*Coventry Races,*" though they still continue to be held on a course in Stoke parish, immediately adjoining Gosford Green. They are now very well attended, and the sport is usually excellent. They take place in the month of March.

INNS.

The three principal Inns in Coventry are the "*King's Head,*" in Smithford-street; the "*Craven Arms,*" High-street; and the *"Castle,"* in Broad-gate.

NEWSPAPERS. There are two newspapers in Coventry, respectively described as "Conservative" and *"*Liberal." The first was established so far back as the year 1741, by a Mr. Jopson, and was then called "Jopson's Coventry Mercury." It subsequently became the property of the late Mr. Rollason, and afterwards of his son, Mr. Charles A. N. Rollason, from whom, in 1836, it was purchased by a company of Conservatives, and thenceforth called the "*Coventry Standard.*" It is still printed and published by Mr. Rollason. The other paper, originally the "*Coventry Herald,*" was established in 1808, by the late Alderman Merridew. In consequence of an alleged departure from its political principles on the part of the *Herald,* commencing with the election in 1826, another paper was started by the Liberal party, in 1828, under the name of the *"Coventry Observer"* An understanding, however, was afterwards come to between the proprietors of the *Observer* and Mr. H. Merridew, the then proprietor of the *Herald;* and ou the latter giving an assurance that the principles. which the *Observer* had been established to support, should thereafter be maintained in the *Herald,* both papers were, in 1830, incorporated under the proprietorship of Mr. H. Merridew, and called the *" Coventry Herald and Observer."* In 1842 the paper was sold, and Mr. John Turner, jun., became the purchaser, and continued the proprietorship till Midsummer, 1846, when, in consequence of ill health, he retired from business, having sold the paper to Mr. C. Bray, by whom it is now carried on.

POPULATION OF COVENTRY. The population of Coventry, as ascertained by the several returns made within the present century, has been as follows: — 1801. —Number of Houses 2,930 Inhabitants 16,049 1811.—Inhabited Houses 3,448

Uninhabited ditto 60

Houses Building 12

Inhabitants 17,923 1821.—Inhabitants 21,242 1831.—Inhabited Houses 5,444

Uninhabited ditto 421

Building 22

Inhabitants 27,070

The population for the different parishes, by the return of 1831, was thus:—St. Michael's, 10,998; Trinity, 9,601; St. John's, 6,471.

1841.—Inhabited Houses 6,526

Uninhabited ditto 597

Building 42

Inhabitants 31,004

St. Michael's and St. John'B Parishes, 19,104; Trinity Parish, 11,900.

Coventry is 94 miles distant from London by railway; 91 by the old coaching road.

Market Days—Wednesday, Friday, and Saturday.

PARLIAMENTARY REPRESENTATION.

The City of Coventry sends two Members to Parliament, a privilege of which the earliest account appears to be towards the close of the 13th century, in the reign of Edward the First; but for several periods, in the course of the two next succeeding centuries, there is no traceable record of the returns.

The elective franchise belongs to the freemen, persons who have served seven years' apprenticeship to one and the same trade within the City and suburbs of Coventry, and not being paupers; and to the £10 voters added by the Reform Act, of whom there are about 600; the freemen being about 3,400 in number, making a total of 4,000 electors.

The City is divided into ten Parliamentary Wards, namely: Gosford-street Ward, Jordanwell Ward, Much Park-street Ward, Bailey-lane Ward, Earl-street Ward, Broad-gate Ward, Smith-ford-street Ward, Spon-street Ward, Crosscheaping Ward, and Bishop-street Ward.

The following is as complete an account of the representation of Coventry from 1295 to the present time as can be given:— 1295 Denikesmus de Coleshill and Richard de Weston 1298 Robert Russell and Robert Kelley 1300 Thomas Bollard and Laurence de Shepway 1302 Ralph To we and John Russell 1306 Alexander Montray and Henry Bury 1315 Richard le Spicer and John Langley 1338 John le Ward and Roger Hunt 1346 John de Fercy and Nicholas de Hunt 1353 Nicholas Mitchell and Richard Stoke 1404 In this year Henry the 4th held a Parliament in the Charter House of Coventry Priory, but there is no record of the names of the Members for this City 1452 William Elton; the name of the other not known 1456 A Parliament held here; the Members for this City not known 1459 Members for this City not known 1467 Henry Botiler; the other not known 1472 Henry Botiler and John Wildnesses 1477 Henry Botiler and John Wildnesses

The writs and returns are lost from 17th of Edward the 4th to 1st of Edward the 6th 1546 Christopher Waren and Henry Porter 1551 James Rogers and John Talbut 1553 John Nethermill and Thomas Bonde Thomas Knevett and Edward Damport 1554 John Throckmorton and John Harris 1555 John Throckmorton and Henry Porter 1557 John Throckmorton and John Tallons 1562 Thomas Dudley and Richard Grafton 1570 Henry Goodere and Edmund Bromwell 1571 Thomas Wright and Edmund Bromwell 1584 Edward Boughton and Thomas Wright 1585 Thomas Sanders and Henry Breeres 1588 Thomas Sanders and Henry Breeres 1592 Thomas Sanders and John Miles 1596 Thomas Sanders and Henry Kirby 1600 Thomas Sanders and Henry Bice 1602 Henry Breeres and John Kogerson 1613 Sir Robert Coke, Knt., and Mr. Hopkins 1619 Sampson Hopkins and Henry Shewall, Aldermen 1622 Sir Edward Coke, Knt., and Henry Harwell, Alderman. —Great contention at this election: the unsuccessful candidate, Sir T. Edmonds, had the support of the Corporation 1625 Henry Harwell, Alderman, and Isaac Walden, Mayor 1627 Richard Green and William Purefoy.—Great contention. The unsuccessful candidates were Mr. Walden and Mr. Potter 1639 William Jesson and Simon Norton, Aldermen 1640 William Jesson and John Barker, Aldermen 1660 John Beak and Richard Hopkins 1672 Sir Clement Fisher, of Packington, and Thomas Flint, of Allesley 1679 Thomas Flint dying, Richard Hopkins was returned, after three days' contest with Sir Robert Townshend: the numbers polled were—For Hopkins, 643; for Townshend, 294

The same year—Richard Hopkins and John Beak 1681 Richard Hopkins and John Stafford 1682 Sir Roger Cave and Sir Thomas Norton 1685 Sir Roger Caye and John Stafford 1689 Richard Hopkins and John Stafford 1690 George Bohun and Thomas Grey 1695 Sir Christopher Hales and Richard Hopkins 1699 Sir Christopher Hales and Richard Hopkins.

1701 The old Members were opposed by H. Neale, Esq., and the Sheriff returned all three. Sir Christopher Hales petitioned the House of Commons, which declared him duly elected, and he brought an action against the Sheriff, damages £600. 1702 Sir Christopher

Hales and Thomas Geary, Tories, were returned; the unsuccessful candidates were Henry Neale and Edward Hopkins, Esqrs. 1705 Sir Christopher Hales and Thomas Geary were opposed by Sir O. Bridgman, and E. Hopkins, Esq. The latter were elected. There was great contention. Hales and Geary were chaired. In consequence of a petition, the election was declared void, and another took place in 1707. 1707 The poll was taken by scores in the Gaol Hall, and at the close Sir O. Bridgman had 693 votes, and Edward Hopkins 673; Sir Christopher Hales 618, and Geary 573. 1708 A severe contest. Sir O. Bridgman and Edward Hopkins, Esq., elected. Sir C. Hales and the Hon. Robert Craven were the unsuccessful candidates. A scrutiny took place, and a petition was presented to the House of Commons against the return, but it was of no avail. 1710 The Tories returned the Hon. Robert Craven and T. Geary, Esq. Craven died soon after, and Sir Christopher Hales was elected in his room. 1713 Sir Christopher Hales and Sir Fulwar Skipwith, Bart. 1714 February. Sir Thomas Samuel, of Upton, Northamptonshire, and Col. Oughton, Whigs, (seconded by the Corporation, or the Low Party,) were elected—Sir Christopher Hales and Sir Fulwar Skipwith, Bart., Tories, (or the High Party,) were the unsuccessful candidates. The numbers polled were—

Oughton, 687—Samuel, 670—Hales, 541— Skipwith, 539. The poll, which was formerly taken at the Gaol, was this year taken in a booth built in front of the Mayor's Parlour, in Cross Cheaping. 1722 Sir Adolphus Oughton and John Neale, Esq., were opposed by Sir Fulwar Skipwith and the Hon. Fulwar Craven. This was a violent contest. Skipwith and Craven petitioned the House against the return of Oughton and Neale, and it was declared an undue election, by their resolutions dated Nov. 20, 1722. Several of the rioters were ordered into custody. On a second contest, Oughton and Neale were again returned. Parliament ordered that the Freemen should be enrolled by the Corporation, and not by the Companies, as

formerly; and declared that the right of election of Citizens to serve in Parliament for the City of Coventry, was in such Freemen as had served seven years apprenticeship to one and the same trade, in the said City, or the Suburbs thereof, and who did not receive alms or weekly charity, such Freemen being duly sworn and enrolled.

1727 Sir A. Oughton, Bart., and J. Neale, Esq., were returned without opposition. 1734 The Right Hon. Earl of Euston, John Neale, Esq., and

Bird, of this City, were candidates— Euston and

Bird were elected. 1741 The Earl of Euston, and John Neale, Esq., of Allesley

Park, were Candidates for the Low Party: for the

High Party, W. Grove, Esq., of this City. Easton and Grove were elected. The poll began on May 5, and ended May 11. Total polled—

Euston, 1299—Grove, 993—Neale, 919.

1747 Lord Petersham and William Grove, Esq., were elected: but Petersham being also elected for St. Edmondsbury, vacated his seat for Coventry, and in the following December a contest ensued between Samuel Greathead, Esq., of Guyscliff, and Robert Bird, Esq., of this City. Greathead was returned. This was a severely-contested election: the party of the latter gentleman, riotously, with drag hooks and red hot chains, pulled down and destroyed the booth. 1754 W. Grove and S. Greathead, Esqrs., were again elected; but were opposed by James Hewitt, Esq., Serjeant-atLaw, a native of Coventry. Greathead, 1194—Grove, 854—Hewitt, 811. On which Hewitt demanded a scrutiny, which was kept open at the Drapers' Hall, but after a few days was abandoned. 1761 The Hon. Andrew Archer and James Hewitt, Esq., were elected. W. Grove, Esq., was unsuccessful. Hewitt, 1079—Archer, 994— Grove, 608. 1766 James Hewitt, Esq., being created a Judge, the Hon. Henry Seymour Conway (son of the Earl of Hertford), was elected in his stead. 1768 The Hon. A. Archer and the Hon. H.

S. Conway again declared themselves, and were elected; but were opposed by Walter Waring, Esq. In this year Lord Archer died, and Alderman Sir Richard Glynn, Bart., of Lon. don, was elected, but was opposed by Thomas Nash, Esq. , seconded by the Low Party. Glynn's chair was decorated with blue satin, lined with white: formerly the chairs were merely dressed with flowers and evergreens. An ox was roasted whole, and also sheep in every Ward. Final close of the poll—

Glynn, 925—Nash, 512.

1773 In January, Sir R Glynn died, and W. Waring, Esq., was elected in his room without opposition. 1774 The Hon. H. S. Conway declined, and Edward Roe Yeo, Esq., of Normanton, in Leicestershire, offered himself, hut was opposed by Thomas Green, Esq. Yeo and Waring were elected. At the close of the poll— 1780 February. Waring died, and John Baker Holroyd, Esq., Lieut.-Colonel of a Regiment of Light Dragoons, quartered in Coventry, was elected in his room, without opposition. 1780 October. Parliament dissolved. An Act of Parliament bad been passed for better regulating the Elections, and swearing the Freemen of Coventry. At this Election violent disturbances took place between the rival parties in front of the booth, in Cross Cheaping, one of which, on the 29th of November, was termed " the Bludgeon Fight." Subsequently Messrs. Noxon and Butler, the two Sheriffs of this City, suffered a short imprisonment in Newgate, for gross partiality. 1783 January. Yeo died, and the Hon. William Seymour Conway, youngest son of the Earl of Hertford, was chosen, without opposition. 1784 April. Parliament dissolved. Lord Sheffield and the Hon. W. S. Conway were proposed by the High Party, and Sir Samson Gideon and John Wilmot, Esq., by the Low Party. After a severe contest of 14 days, the partisans of Sheffield and Conway became riotous, and on the morning of the 13th of April came with hammers, saws, &c, concealed under their clothes, and when the Sheriffs opened the poll, immediately destroyed the booth, which the Sheriffs again rebuilt. On the 15th, at midnight, Sheffield and Conway, finding they had no chance of success, left the City, on which Gideon and Wilmot were declared duly elected, and on April 21 were chaired. 1790 June. Lord Eardley and Mr. Wilmot, his brother-inlaw, were elected. Mr. Bird, of Coventry, was the unsuccessful candidate. The poll lasted nine days, and terminated as follows:— 1796 Mr. W. Bird, of Coventry, and Nathaniel Jefferys, of London, Esq., were returned. John Petre and W. Berners, Esqrs., relinquished all opposition on the morning of the poll. 1802 Nathaniel Jefferys, Esq., and Francis W. Barlow, Esq., of Middlethorp, near York, were elected. At the close of the poll, July 17, the numbers were—

Barlow, 1197—Jefferys, 1190—Bird, 1182—

Moore, 1152. Total polled, 2369.

A Petition was presented to the House of Commons by Messrs. Bird and Moore, in November, 1802, complaining of an undue election.

Lord Eardley and Mr. Wilmot

Mr. W. Bird

1399 1126 1803 On March 30, 1803, N. Jefferys, Esq., being found disqualified by a Committee of the House of Commons, a new election took place, when Peter Moore, Esq., became the representative of the City. George Frederic Stratton, Esq., was the unsuccessful candidate. The numbers polled were—

Moore, 1294— Stratton, 1146.

A petition against Moore's return was presented to the

House of Commons; but the house declared him duly elected.

1805 In consequence of the death of Captain Barlow, a new election took place, when William Mills, Esq., was returned.

1806 November 12. P. Moore and W. Mills, Esqrs., were re-elected without opposition. 1807 May. P. Moore and W. Mills, Esqrs., re-elected. They were opposed by H. C. Montgomery and M. Sliawe, Esqrs. Close of the poll:—

Moore, 1464—Mills, 1464—Montgomery, 703

—Shawe, 694.

1812 W. Mills resigned, and P. Moore

and Joseph Butterworth, Esqrs., were elected. William George Harris, Esq., was a candidate, but resigned.

1818 June. P. Moore, Edward Ellice, and J. Butterworth, Esqrs., were the candidates. The Corporation exerted the utmost of their influence in favour of the latter gentleman, but without success. At the close of the poll the numbers were—

Moore, 1180—Ellice, 1000—Butterworth, 624.

1820 Peter Moore and Edward Ellice were opposed by William Cobbett. Scenes of tumult and violence characterized the whole of this election.

Close of the Poll (the seventh day).

Ellice, 1474 Moore, 1422 Cobbett, 517

Total polled 2016.

1826 June. Advantage having been taken of the unpopularity of Moore and Ellice with the weavers, on the free trade question, and also of the hostility of the radical (or Cobbett) party, Messrs. Fyler and Heathcote were brought forward, who succeeded in defeating the former members, after much excitement and violence. At the close of the poll (June 19) the numbers were—

The successful candidates were supported by the Corporation. The return was petitioned against by the defeated party, but the members were permitted to retain their seats.

1830 Mr. Heathcote declining to offer himself again, Messrs. Fyler, Ellice, and Spooner, were the only Candidates, and the contest terminated in a few hours, Mr. Spooner having retired.

Heathcote

Fyler.

Ellice.

Moore

1536

1522

1242

1182

Total number polled 2763 1831 Parliament was dissolved by Earl Grey's Ministry, on the question of Parliamentary Reform. Mr. Fyler was opposed on various grounds by the influential part of the Reformers, who invited Mr. Henry Lyttou Bulwer to take the field. He

accepted their invitation, and was successful. At the close of the poll, May 4:—

Ellice 1663

Bulwer 1564

Fyler 1115 1832 Parliament dissolved to give effect to the new franchise created by the Reform Act. Candidates—Edward Ellice, H. h. Bulwer, T. B. Fyler, and Morgan Thomas; the two latter Conservatives. The intensity of the opposition gave rise to much personal violence on both sides at this election, which took place on the 10th of December, sometimes called "The Bloody Tenth," as expressive of the scenes of turbulence which prevailed.

Close of the poll.

Ellice 1607

Bulwer 1613

Fyler 371

Thomas 366

The unsuccessful party petitioned against the return,

but failed in the attempt to unseat their opponents.

Mr. Ellice vacated his seat in consequence of having been appointed Secretary-at-War in Earl Grey's Ministry. In presenting himself before the electors, he was again opposed by Mr. Thomas. A son of Mr.

Cobbett was also put in nomination, but did not appear.

Ellice 1502

Thomas 1208

Cobbett 89 1835 Formation of a Conservative Administration by Sir R. Peel. Messrs. Ellice and Bulwer were on this occasion once more met by Mr. Thomas; and the Radicals, having formed a strong prejudice against Mr. Ellice, brought forward William Williams to oppose him. Mr. Bulwer however, having, in consequence of this movement, retired, left the field to be contested by the remaining candidates. By the electioneering tactics of the Radicals, 500 or 600 electors of the Conservative party were induced to vote not only for Mr. Thomas, but for Mr. Williams also, who was consequently returned and placed at the head of the poll, which took place on the 8th of January:—

Williams 1865
Ellice 1601
Thomas 1566 1837 Death of William IV. Candidates—the late Members, Ellice and Williams; Conservative Candidates, Morgan
Thomas and J. D. H. Hill; Chartist, John Bell.
Close of the Poll, July 24.

Ellice 1778
Williams 1748
Thomas 1511
Hill 1393
Bell 44 1841 The defeat of the Whig Government on the Corn, Sugar, and Timber Duties, induced them to dissolve the Parliament. Candidates—Messrs. Ellice and Williams, who were opposed on the part of the Conservatives by Thomas Weir. Close of the poll, June 26:—

Williams, 1871—Ellice, 1826—Weir, 1286.
T
1847 A natural dissolution of Parliament. Up to a short time before the election, there appeared little reason to expect any opposition to the old members; but, at almost the eleventh hour, the Conservatives introduced Mr. George James Turner, a Chancery Barrister, to oppose Mr. Williams, a section of whose particular supporters, by their unfriendly bearing, if not absolute hostility, towards the old Liberal party with whom Mr. Ellice was more particularly identified, had, to some extent, alienated that spirit of co-operation which, on former occasions, had largely contributed to Mr. Williams's success. The consequence was, that Mr. Williams lost his seat, the numbers being, at the close of the poll, on the 29th of July, as follows:—

Ellice 2901
Turner 1754
Williams 1633
The number of voters on the register for this year was 4043.

REMARKABLE OCCURRENCES IN COVENTRY. 1016.—The St. Osburg nunnery was destroyed by Edric the Traitor, who in that year invaded Mercia, and destroyed many towns therein. 1043.—About this period Leofric, Earl of Mer-

cia, and his Countess Godiva, founded the Great Monastery in Coventry. 1057.—Leofric, Earl of Mercia, died. The Countess Godiva died some years afterwards, and both of them were buried in the church porch belonging to the Monastery which they had founded.
Id 1218, the Charter for a yearly fair to continue eight days was granted by Henry 3rd.

In 1344, by virtue of letters patent, granted by King Edward the 3rd, a Municipal Corporation, consisting of Mayor and Bailiffs, was constituted in Coventry. The name of the first Mayor was John Ward.

Sept., 1397.—In the reign of Richard 2nd, the preliminaries and " note of preparation" took place for a single combat to be fought on Gosford Green, between the Duke of Hereford (afterwards Henry 4th), and the Duke of Norfolk (Thomas Mowbray). The former, it was said, betrayed a private conversation, in which Mowbray is represented to have used several expressions of a treasonable nature. The accusation was denied, and Mowbray demanded the privilege of acquitting himself by single combat. Each of the Dukes, agreeably to the laws of chivalry, threw down his glove, which was taken up and sealed before the King (a circumstance which was supposed to prevent all future denial of the challenge.) The King appointed Coventry for the place of combat, and caused a vast and magnificent theatre to be erected for that purpose on Gosford Green. The rival Dukes made every requisite preparation, and particularly in the essential article of armour, which in those days was uncommonly splendid and expensive, usually inlaid with gold and silver, and ornamented with most elegant figures and devices. The combatants placed their reliance totally on the skill of the armourer, and cleared themselves by oath from holding any commerce with incantations, or rendering their armour or bodies invulnerable by any charm. Be their cause ever so bad, they must determine to die like good christians, and they therefore disavowed all dependance on the power of Satan, and supplicated the prayers of

all pious spectators:— "Add proof unto my armour with thy prayers, And with thy blessings steel my lance's point." Henry, Duke of Hereford, advanced from Baginton Castle towards the place appointed upon his white courser, barded with blue and green velvet, beautifully embroidered with swans and antelopes, and armed at all points. Thomas Mowbray, Duke of Norfolk, set out from Caludon Castle on a horse barded with crimson velvet, and embroidered with lions of silver and mulberry leaves (alluding to the name of *Mowbray*—mulberry.)

"At the fime appointed, the King came to Coventrie," says Hollinshead, "in great arraie, accompanied with the lords and gentlemen of their linages. The Duke of Hereford armed himself in his tent, that was set up neere to the lists; and the Duke of Norfolke put on his armour betwixt the gate and the barrier of the towne, in a beautifull house, having a fair perclois of wood towards the gate, that none might see what was doono within the house.

"The Duke of Aumarle that daie being High Constable of England, and the Duke of Surrie, Marshall, placed themselves betwixt them, well armed and appointed. About the hour of prime the Duke of Hereford came to the barriers of the lists on a white courser. The constable and marshall came and demanded of him what he was? He answered,' I am Henrie of Lancaster, Duke of Hereford, which am come hither to doo mine endeavor against Thomas Mowbraie, Duke of Norfolke, as a traitor.' Then incontinentlie he sware upon the Holie Evangelists, that his quarrell was true and just. Then putting down his vizor, he decended from his horse, and, with speare in hand, set him downe in a chaire of green velvet at the end of the lists, and there reposed himselfe, abiding the comming of his adversaria.

"Soone after him, entered into the field, with great triumph, King Richard, accompanied with all the peeres of the realme, and above ten thousand men in armour, least some fraie or tumult might rise amongst his nobles.

"The Duke of Norfolke hovered on

horseback at the entrance of the lists; and when he had made his oth before the constable that his quarrell was just, he entered the field manfullie, saieing aloud, ' God aid him that hath the right;' and then he departed from his horse and sate himself downe in his chaire, which was of crimson velvet. The Lord Marshall viewed their speares, to see that they were of equal length. Then the Herald proclaimed that the traverses and chaires should be removed, commanding them to mount on horsebacke and address themselves to the battell and combat.

"The Duke of Hereford was quicklie horsed, and closed his bavier, and cast his speare into the rest; and when the trumpet sounded, set forward couragiouslie towards his opponent six or seven pases. The Duke of Norfolke was not fullie set forward, when the King cast downe his warder, and the Heralds cried ' Ho, ho.' Then the King caused their speares to be taken from them, and commanded them to repairs againe to their chairs, where they remained two long houres, while the King and his counsell deliberatlie consulted what order was best to be had in so weightie a cause."

The result of this deliberation was to prohibit the combat, together with a sentence against the Duke of Hereford to depart the realm, and not to return again for the term of ten years; and that the Duke of Norfolk, because he had sown sedition, should depart the realm for life. The term of Hereford's banishment was subsequently mitigated to sis years.

In 1404 Henry 4th held a Parliament in the great chamber of the Priory, in this City, at which no lawyer was suffered to be present. It was styled *Parlmmentum Indoctorum,* from its inveteracy to the clergy; whence it was also called the *Laymen's Parliament.*

In 1406 John Botoner, the Mayor, caused the streets of Coventry to be paved.

In 1411 John Horneby, the Mayor, arrested the Prince (afterwards Henry 5th), at the Priory, in this City.

In 1422 *the first Cross was built in Cross Cheaping.* Ia the same year, according to one of the old city manuscripts, "A dooke stool (ducking pond) was made upon Cheylesmore Green, to punish scolders and chiders, as ye law wylls."

In 1429 bells were first hung in St. Michael's steeple.

In 1436 King Henry 6th came to Coventry, and kept Christmas at Kecilworth.

In 1446 John Heires and William Lingham were hanged for robbing St. Mary's Hall. In the same year a Bishop was installed in Coventry.

In 1450 Henry 6th heard mass in St. Michael's Church, and presented a golden cloth.

In 1451 the same King granted the Charter giving this City a County and other privileges.

In 1453 King Henry and Queen Margaret came to Coventry, and slept at the Priory.

In 1459 another Parliament was held at the Priory, by Henry 6th, which was called *Parliamentum Diabolicum,* on account of the multitude of attainders passed against Richard Duke of York and others.

In 1465 Edward 4th and his Queen kept Christmas here.

Ih 1468 the Earl of Rivers and his son were beheaded on Gosford Green.

In 1469 one Elipane was beheaded, and his head set on a pole on Bablake-gate.

In 1471 the leaders of an insurrection in London were beheaded in Coventry.

In 1474 Prince Edward for the first time came to this City, and was presented with a cup and JE100.

In 1477 Prince Edward again came to Coventry, and was made a brother of different Guilds. He kept his Court at Cheylesmore. The same year the custom of riding the liberties of the City was introduced.

In 1480 there was a tumult amongst the inhabitants of this City: they rang the common bell, and opened a pasture which had been for some time before enclosed. In the same year the old sword and the best mace were stolen from the Mayor's house.

In 1483 Richard 3rd came to Coventry at the festival of Corpus Christi, to see the plays; and kept his Christmas at Kenil worth.

In 1485 Henry 7th came to this City, after his victory over Richard 3rd at Bosworth Field, and lodged at the house of Robert Onley, the Mayor, who presented the King with a cup and £100, and in return received the honour of knighthood.

In 1487 Thomas Harrington, of Oxford, was brought here and beheaded on the conduit opposite the Bull, for having called himself the son of the Duke of Clarence.

In 1492 Henry 7th, with his Queen, came to see the plays performed by the Grey Friars.

In 1495 Sir Henry Mumford and Sir Robert Mallerie were beheaded under Binley Gallows, for treason. Mumford's head was placed on Bablake-gate, and Mallerie's on Bishopgate.

In 1497 Prince Arthur came to Coventry, and was presented with a cup and £100.

In 1499 Henry 7th and his Queen came to this City, and were made a brother and sister of Trinity Gild.

In 1510 the *old* cross was taken down. In the same year Henry 8th and his Queen came to Coventry to witness the pageants, and afterwards proceeded to the Priory. Also in this year Joan Ward was burnt in the Little Park for heresy.

In 1512 a hundred men were raised in Coventry for foreign military service.

In 1519 Robert Sikeby was burnt for denying " the real presence."

In 1522 two men named Pratt and South were arrested here for treason. They confessed it was also their intention to have put the Mayor and Aldermen to death and robbed St Mary's Hall. They were afterwards "hanged, drawn, and quartered," and their heads and limbs exposed on four of the City gates.

On Lammas day, 1524, the inhabitants pulled down the gates and hedges of some ground that had been enclosed. The people within the city closed New Gate against the Chamberlains and their company, and the Mayor was sent a prisoner to London, and removed from his office.

In 1525 the Princess Mary came to Coventry to witness the Mercers' pageant, and remained two days at the Priory.

In 1541 the Mayor laid the first stone of the *new* Cross in Cross Cheaping. It was finished in 1544.

In 1550 the Magistrates of Coventry had a sale of wood in the Park, and sold the pales. The Park was then made a pasture.

In 1555, Feb. 8th, Mr. Laurence Saunders was burned in the Little Park for heresy. About the same time Robert Glover, of Mancetter, and Cornelius Bongay, of Coventry, were also burnt on similar charges.

In 1560 the Boys' Hospital, at Bablake, was built

In the beginning of 1563 wheat sold at 8s. a strike, but in the end of the same year it had fallen to Is. 2d. the strike.

On the 17th of August, 1565, Queen Elizabeth came to Coventry, where she was splendidly received by the Mayor and Citizens, with a variety of shows and entertainments.

In 1566 Mary Queen of Scots was confined as a prisoner in the Mayoress's Parlour, in this City.

In 1567 the Park was granted in *fee ferme* to this City.

In 1569 Mary Queen of Scots was again imprisoned in Coventry, at the Bull Inn.

The same year the Register Books of St. Michael's Church were burnt, because they contained some marks ef Popery.

In 1574 the Mayor's Parlour was erected in Cross Cheaping.

In 1575 the old Coventry Play of " Hock Tuesday" was performed before Queen Elizabeth, for her entertainment while at Kenilworth Castle.

In 1586, in consequence of a great scarcity of provisions, every man, woman, and child, in this City, was numbered, and were found to amount to 6,502 persons.

In 1603, April 3, the Princess Elizabeth, eldest daughter of James I., accompanied by other persons of distinction, came to Coventry from Combe Abbey. She was met by the Mayor and Corporation at Stoke Green, and received by the various Companies, and after having heard a sermon at St. Michael's Church, dined with the Mayor, who presented her with a silver cup at the City's expense. The same year the plague raged so dreadfully in Coventry, that 494 persons died of it.

V

In 1605 two fat oxen, worth £18, were given to the Princess Elizabeth as a present from this City.

In 1608 Bablake Church was repaired; the picture of a Dead Christ being taken from the Cross, was removed thence, and the King's Arms placed in its stead.

In 1611 Prince Henry, with a train of nobility, came to this City, and were entertained at St. Mary's Hall. £50 was given to the Prince as a present.

In 1613 the long gallery on the south side of St. Michael's Church was built; it cost £59. 16s.

In August, 1616, King James I. visited Coventry with a numerous train of nobility, and in expectation of this visit, most of the houses and gates had been painted black and white. There was a grand procession of the Mayor and Corporation, and a cup of pure gold, which cost £160, weighing 45 ounces, was presented to his Majesty, who promised to drink out of it wherever he went, and ordered it to be put amongst the royal plate. The King slept at the White Friars.

In 1622 the Mayor planted 250 young trees in the Park.

In 1626 the two Chamberlains paid a fine of £20, for making a smaller feast at Lammas than their predecessors.

In 1627 the Mount in the Park was raised, and trees planted in the middle of the Mount.

In 1629 a Pillory was erected in Cross Cheaping.

In 1632 the Swanswell Water Works were constructed.

In 1635 Old Parr passed through Coventry, aged 152 years.

In the same year the first tax for ship-money was paid in Coventry.

In 1642 the New Buildings were erected on the site of the Priory.

In 1647 the Scotch Army under the Duke of Hamilton being beaten, several hundred prisoners were brought to this City, and confined in Leather Hall, Bablake Church, Spon Tower, Grey Friars' Tower, and other places.

In 1648 a riot took place between the soldiers and tha butchers.

In 1650 Charles II. came into England, and Coventry was again fortified, and a regiment of infantry raised for its defence.

1662. On the 24th August, this year, the Rev. Dr. Obadiah Grew, Vicar of St. Michael's, and the Rev. Dr. John Bryan, Vicar of Trinity, and Mr. Basnet, Lecturer at both Churches, were simultaneously ejected from their livings under the Act of Uniformity. Dr. Grew evinced strong attachment to Coventry, and repeated his visits and preachings here at several periods afterward. He endured six months' imprisonment in gaol on account of his Nonconformist principles; and died 22nd Oct., 1689.

In 1674 the six bells of St. Michael's Church were cast into eight. In this year part of Trinity spire was taken down and rebuilt.

In September, 1682, the Duke of Monmouth came to Coventry, and lodged at the Star Inn, in Earl-street.

In September, 1687, King James II. came to Coventry, when he was received by the Mayor, who presented him with a gold cup, weighing 3 lbs., which cost £167. 7s. 6d.

In 1688, December 11, the Princess Ann of Denmark, with attendants, came to Coventry for security.

On the 5th June, 1690, King William came to Coventry, on his journey to Ireland. He dined at Packington Hall, and thence proceeded to Lichfield, where he slept the same night.

In 1694 the inhabitants of this City were numbered, on account of a payment which was levied by Parliament on births and burials; the population amounted to 6,710.

In 1696 Samuel Smith, a mercer, introduced the art of weaving tammies into this City..

In 1698 the Register of St. Michael's Parish, kept in a cupboard in the vestry, was accidentally destroyed by fire. In the same year the common Gaol of this City was taken down, and rebuilt at an expense of £350.

In 1711 party politics ran high, and a plot was laid to seize the Sword and Mace on the 1st November, when the Mayor (Joseph Eburne) came to be sworn in at St. Mary's Hall. The Sword and Mace were therefore deposited at a house in Fleet-street, where, in the open street, the ceremony of swearing-in the Mayor was suddenly gone through; and in consequence of subsequent similar designs during this mayoralty, the Sword and Mace were privately conveyed in a basket of wool to Canley, near this City.

In 1719 the Women's Market was removed from the Great Butcher-row to its present situation.

In 1723 St. Michael's Parish contained 1237 houses, and Trinity Parish 697.

In 1734 Thomas Wildey, a woolcomber, murdered his aunt Susannah Wall, and Ann Shenton her daughter, who kept the White Lion, in Smithford-street.

On Monday, July 20, 1741, the Coventry Mercury newspaper was first printed in this City by Mr. Jopson.

In 1745 a company of soldiers was raised in this City, to resist the Scotch Rebels.

By Bradford's survey in 1748-9,Coventry appears to have contained 2,065 houses, and 12,117 inhabitants.

In August, 1755, horse races were instituted in Coventry Park, S. Greatbead, Esq., steward.

1756.—At this time, (in the month of May,) as appears from the journal of John Hewitt, Mayor, a shrewd and expert Magistrate, there were 126 Licensed Victuallers in Coventry, at whose houses above 600 soldiers were billeted. There were 16 at the "White Bear," High-street; 14 at the " Rose and Crown," High-street; 14 at the "Black Lion," High-street; 14 at the " Coach and Horses," Muchford-street; 12 at the "Bull's Head," Bishop-street; 12 at the " Horse Sboe,"Sponend; 10 at the " Nag's Head," Spon-end; 10 at the " Eagle and Child," Fleet-street; and 10 officers at the " King's Head," Smithford.street. At the other houses they were quartered in numbers of from two to eight each.

In the month of September, in the same year, there were symptoms of rioting on account of the high price of provisions, and a number of colliers entered the town from Bed worth. On this occasion the Mayor, John Hewitt, caused an abstract of the laws against forestalling to be printed and circulated.

In 1757, in the months of April and June, two soldiers were shot for desertion, under the Park wall, near the end of Little Park-street.

In 1762 New Gate was taken down.

In 1763 Swine's Cross, which stood in Bishop-street, opposite Silver-street, was taken down.

In 1765, on the night of Friday, the 18th of March, Thomas Edwards, a farmer, was murdered near Whoberly, on his return from this City, by Moses Baker, a weaver of Coventry, and two Dragoons named Drury and Leslie, who had come from their quarters at Warwick.

In this year Gosford Gate was taken down.

In 1767 Spon Bridge was built.

The following is a card of the Coventry Races for the same year:— "COVENTRY RACES, 1767.

"Wednesday, Adgcst 12.—Members of the City's Pane,

Fifty Pounds.

Edward Popham, Esqr's, chesnut horse Lath,

5 yrs. old.—Rider: John South 1 1

Mr. Archer's bay horse, Honest Farmer.—Miles

Thistlethwait 2 3

Edmund Turner, Esqr's, chesnut borse. Spot.—

Robert Wilson 3 2

"thursday, August 13.—The City's Purse of Fifty Pounds.

Dr. Huddlestone's chesnut horse, Galin, 4 yrs 3 1 1

Mr. Nutt's bay horse, Honest Billy dr

Mr. Payne's bay horse, Sloven

Daniel Miret 12 2

"Friday, August 14.—The Chamberlains' Purse of Fifty Pounds.

Mr. Nutt's bay horse, Early Thistlethwait 1 1

Mr. Lenton's black horse, Black Prince Fisher 2 2

Mr. Jordan's c. horse, Schoolboy J. Ives 0 0"

In 1771 Spon Gate was taken down. In the same year Grey Friars' Spire was repaired, and a gilt ball and vane placed on its summit

In March, 1772, one Mary Cloes, of Gosford street, nearly opposite Newcourt, was burnt to death by spontaneous combustion. She lived in a room with a brick floor, and had been confined to her bed some time by illness, caused by intemperance. The bed on which she lay had but one curtain, and stood next the window, the fire-place being on the opposite side of the room. The evening before the accident, she was left with only two bits of coal in the grate and a rushlight on a chair at the head of her bed. Smoke being seen to issue from her door the next morning, the door was burst open; and her remains lay on the floor, almost reduced to a cinder, while the furniture and bed clothes were scarcely damaged. The deceased was so excessively addicted to dram-drinking, that she occasionally drank a quart of rum, or of aniseed water, daily; and thus filling her veins with spirits, she became inflammable as a lamp. The belief is, that she rolled out of bed, took fire from the candle, and thus was totally burnt, her thighs and one leg excepted; and nothing was left but her bones, which were in a complete state of calcination.

On the night of November 2, in the same year, Charles Pinchbeck, keeper of the Stoke toll-gate, near Binley, was robbed and murdered in his own house by two burglars named Farn and Howe.

In the same year the Gaol of this City, being in a decayed state, and constructed upon a plan too confined, was rebuilt upon an enlarged scale.

On the 20th of May, 1773, the river Sherborne overflowed, and laid part of the city nearly seven feet under water.

On the 24th of November, the same year, Mr. Siddons, the tragedian, was married to Miss Kemble at St. Michael's Church.

In 1774 the eight bells of St. Michael's Church were recast into ten, by Pack and Chapman, and hung by R. Turner, of London. The weight amounted to 6 tons, 18 cwt. 2 qrs. 11 lbs.

In 1779 a new set of Chimes was placed in St. Michael's steeple, made by Worton of Birmingham, at an expense of £300.

In 1780 Messrs. Noxon and Butler, the two Sheriffs of this City, were sent to Newgate, and suffered a short imprisonment there, for misconduct at the election of Members of Parliament. The same year took place the " Bludgeon Fight" between the rival electioneering parties, in front of the booth in Cross-cheaping. It was at this election that a number of unqualified persons were admitted to the freedom by the Corporation, on condition of voting for the Corporation candidates. These surreptitious voters were called " Mushroom Freemen."

In October, 1781, Grey Friars' Gate was taken down.

In 1783 a double row of houses, at the south-west angle of St. Michael's Churchyard, was taken down.

In 1785 the County Hall was built.

In the same year Sunday Schools were formed in Coventry. The first in connexion with a place of worship was that established at West-orchard Chapel, of which the Rev. George Burder was then minister. This was followed almost immediately by one at St. Michael's Church. The members of the Church of England and the Dissenters were, at that period, united in Coventry in the promotion of Sunday Schools.

In 1786 the east end of Trinity Church was re-built. The same year St. Michael's Church was broken into, and the Communion-plate and other articles stolen from the vestry.

In 1787 St. Michael's Churchyard was enlarged opposite the County Hall.

In the same year the Golden Horse public house was set on fire by Mary Felkin, who was convicted and executed for the offence. The Golden Horse was then situated in Pepperlane, on part of the site of the present Gaol.

In 1788 the Canal Office was built.

In 1793 the Barracks were built on the site of the Bull Inn.

In 1794 the great wooden framework for the bells of St. Michael's tower was constructed, and the bells re-hung. The expense was estimated at £3752.

In the same year the street on St. John's Bridges was widened, for which purpose the front of the Free School was taken down and rebuilt.

In February, 1795, the Park began to be enclosed.

In 1797 an association of the inhabitants of this City was formed into two troops of cavalry and three companies of infantry.

In February, 1798, a soup institution was first established in Coventry.—In the same year this City and neighbourhood subscribed several thousand pounds in aid of Government, to prosecute the war.

In September, 1800, food riots took place in Coventry in consequence of the dearness of provisions. The disturbance was quelled by the military, with the magistrates and the "Coventry Volunteers."

In 1801 the Act of Parliament for uniting the Parishes for the purpose of providing for the poor was passed.

By the census taken the same year, Coventry was reported to contain 2930 houses, and 16,049 inhabitants. The County of the City 5,547 inhabitants.

On September 3, 1802, Lord Nelson, accompanied by Sir William and Lady Hamilton and other friends, arrived in this City, and alighting at the King's Head Inn, met with the hearty acclamations of the inhabitants. The Mayor and Corporation waited on the gallant hero, who gave them a polite reception.

In January, 1805, a company of volunteers was raised in this City, to join the First Regiment of Warwickshire Volunteer Infantry.

In 1807 the bells in St. Michael's steeple were re-hung, on an improved plan, upon the framework erected within the tower in 1794. The tenor, weigh-

ing upwards of 32 cwt., was re-cast by Mr. Briant, of Hertford.

On the 18th of September, 1807, the Prince of Wales and the Duke of Sussex passed through this City on their route from Ragley, the seat of the Marquis of Hertford, to Combe Abbey, the seat of the Earl of Craven. Here they were visited a few days afterwards by a deputation from the Corporation of Coventry, presenting " a loyal and dutiful address," W to which a gracious answer was given, and the deputation, consisting of the Mayor, (Basil Goode, Esq. ,) with four Aldermen and the Town Clerk, were regaled with a sumptuous repast. The Prince gave a donation of 100 guineas, and the Duke a donation of 40 guineas, to be distributed by the Corporation, and the same was given to four public charities in the proportion of 35 guineas to each.

In the same year a second volunteer company was raised in this City, to join the First Regiment of Warwickshire Volunteer Infantry.

On the 24th of November, 1808, Louis the 18th of France and his suite passed through this City.

In 180!) the two companies of Coventry Volunteers, with their Regiment, entered into the First Regiment of Warwickshire Local Militia.

On the 25th of October, 1809, a general festival took place in this City in celebration of the *jubilee,* or fiftieth anniversary of the accession of George the 3rd. A public subscription, amounting to £756. 5s., was raised and distributed to families, comprising 11,000 individuals, in allowances of bread, meat, and ale. The debtors in the gaol were released; the criminal prisoners were supplied with roast beef and 5s. each. The Bablake Boys had roast beef, plum pudding, and 6d. each. The old women at Ford's, and the old men at Bablake, Hospitals, had 2s. each; and a like sum was given to the Blue Coat Girls. The poor at the House of Industry were also suitably entertained by the liberality of Lord Grey and the officers of the 4th Warwickshire Regiment of Local Militia; and a bountiful supply of good fare was given to the soldiers of the 14th

Light Dragoons, head quarters of which regiment then lay in the Coventry Barracks. A great dinner of the Corporation took place at St. Mary's Hall. Sheep roasting was general, and in tbe evening a grand display of fireworks and bonfires was made in Cross-cheaping and other parts of the town.

In 1812 an Act of Parliament was obtained "for improving the public roads in and through the City of Coventry," and authorizing toll gates to be erected at its different extremities to meet the expense. Under this Act Hertford-street was formed, having been commenced immediately on the passing of the Act, previous to which time all the coaching and carriage traffic in the direction of Warwick, was carried on through the narrow and dangerous avenue Grey Friars-lane.

1815. This year the Rev. J. Davis, accompanied by the parish officers and others," walked the bounds" of the Holy Trinity parish, on his induction to the vicarage. Mr. Davis had officiated in the same Church from the year 1811.

In the same year (1815) the Prince Regent (late George the Fourth), visited Combe Abbey, the seat of Earl Craven, on which occasion the Mayor, and a deputation from the Corporation of Coventry, waited on his Royal Highness with a loyal and dutiful address. The Prince Regent, in return, conferred the honour of knighthood upon the Mayor, Mr. Skears Rew.

In 1816 the Chantry Orchard (now Chantry Place), began to be built upon. The foundations of the first eight houses were laid by Mr. A. Sprigg, on the 8th of May, and by the Midsummer following they were inhabited. The Chantry Orchard now contains above 600 inhabitants.

This year 27 feet of St. Michael's Church spire was taken down and rebuilt.

1817. On the 27th February this year, Thomas Lawson, butcher, was killed in his bed, by the falling of his house, in the Great Butcher-row.

In April, Charles Sanders was executed at Warwick, for the murder of an old man uamed Rogers, at Keresley.

At the Great Fair, in the month of June this year, a bear was shot on Grey Friars'-green, by order of the Magistrates, it having been previously shaved and tortured by some showpeople, in order to practice an imposition on the public, by exhibiting it under the name of the " Polo-Savage." 1818. In the month of August the weathercock of St. Michael's Church was regilt and replaced.

In the month of September this year, William Law was killed by a man named Jackson, of Foleshill, in a quarrel on the Warwick-road, near Coventry, when returning from Kenilworth Statutes.

1819. 37th October, Prince Leopold (now King of the Belgians), passed through Coventry, and was presented with the freedom of the City. 1820. This year the west side of " Broad-gate," a short narrow street, but a great thoroughfare and seat of trade, was pulled down, together with several houses on the north side of Smithford-street, and the whole thrown open, making a direct communication into Hertford-street, and thence to the Warwick turnpike road. In excavating the foundations of the site of the old Broad-gate, the cellaring exhibited some fine specimens of massive stone arches, remains of the Grey Friars' Monastery, on the precincts of the ancient manor of Cheylesmore.

"Union-street" and " White Friars'-street" were built the same year.

1821. April 18, Edward Bradshaw was executed on Whitley Common, for burglary at the Punch Bowl public house, Spon-end, and cutting and wounding Mr. Lines, the landlord.

Moore and Batcher were executed after the Lammas assizes, the same year, on Whitley Common, for burglary and attempt to murder, at Mr. Owen's farm, Longford.

The first public Gas-works were this year erected in Coventry.

1828. This year the fields lying between Swanswell pool and Primrose-hill began to be converted into building land. The first house erected in Hill Field, or, as it is now called, "New Town,"

is situate in King William-street, a row of houses adjoining the field,in Harnal-lane, having been reared a short time before. There are now about 2000 inhabitants in this district. 1829. The ball and fan of Grey Friars' or Christ Church spire was taken down and re-gilt. The erection of the Church was commenced in this year. 1830. May 31, Mr. Green ascended from Coventry in his balloon.

At Coventry Fair, June 18, Mr. Green again rose in his balloon from Grey Friars' Green, skimmed over the tops of the houses for a short distance, and came in contact with a chimney near Gosford-bridge, when he alighted.

In the month of November the same year, a new conductor was affixed to St. Michael's steeple from the summit to the base, on which occasion the weathercock was temporarily taken down.

1831. August 11th, Mary Ann Higgins was executed on Whitley Common for murdering her uncle by means of poison, an old man of the same name, residing in Spon street.

The same year the old Bridewell, near Bablake Church, was taken down, and the establishment consolidated with the Gaol.

On the 7th of November this year, a meeting of ribbon weavers was held in the morning on the subject of wages, and in the course of collecting a meeting for the evening, a party entered the factory of Josiah Beck, down a yard in New-buildings, where the machinery was worked by steam power, and set fire thereto. Several persons were apprehended and tried for the offence, two of whom, named Sparkes and Burbery, were condemned to death, but their sentences were afterwards commuted to transportation for life. The factory destroyed as above stated was the first steam power establishment in the silk trade introduced into Coventry.

In 1835 the Municipal Corporations Act was passed, and came into effect January 1st, 1836: on the 7th of January the Insignia of Office and Civic Regalia were transferred by George Eld, Esq. , the last Mayor under the old system, to Henry Cadwallader Adams, Esq., the first Mayor under the new system in

Coventry.

1839. On the 1st of November this year Adelaide Queen Dowager passed through Coventry on hsr way from Gopsal Hall, the seat of Earl Howe, to Warwick Castle. "The Mayor, Aldermen, and Burgesses," forming the Corporation of Coventry, assembled on this occasion, and, proceeding to the Boundary of the County of the City on the Leicester-road, met her Majesty there, and accompanied her in procession to the limit of the Coventry jurisdiction on the Warwick side.

In 1842 the New Boundary Act was passed, putting an end to the ancient jurisdiction of Coventry, and assigning a new Boundary to the City.

In 1844 the Waterworks, the Cemetery, and the Coventry Improvement Acts were passed.

In 1846 the large Nursery Ground at Spon-end was laid out for building purposes; and in 1847 the first houses were erected.

EMINENT NATIVES OF COVENTRY.

Coventry has given birth to several persons of eminence in days gone by.

Vincent of Coventry, who lived in the early part of the 13th century, was distinguished as being the first of the Franciscans who applied himself to academical studies. He was brought up at Cambridge, where he became a public professor, wrote an exposition of the mass, and other theological works.

William Maklesfield was a native of Coventry. He was a celebrated scholar in his day, and was general of the order of Dominicans.

John Bird was educated as a Carmelite at Oxford, and subsequently became bead and last provincial of his order. His obsequiousness to Henry the 8th, by preaching against the Pope's primacy, obtained for him in succession the bishoprics of Bangor and Chester; but yielding further to the pursuit of personal interest and aggrandisement, he again became an instrument of the papacy in the reign of Queen Mary.

John Grant was a native of Coventry, whom it is better to describe as notorious rather than celebrated. He was executed in London in 1606 as a conspirator, after having been tried for stealing horses from the stables of several gentlemen in this neighbourhood, for the purpose of carrying off the Princess Elizabeth, when on a visit to Lord Harrington's, at Coombe Abbey.

Humphrey Wanley, the son of Nathaniel Wanley, Vicar of Trinity Church, and born about 1672, was distinguished as a scholar and antiquary, though in his youth he had been put to a mechanical trade. He was sent to St. Edmund's Hall, Oxford, and afterwards appointed librarian to the Earl of Oxford. At the desire of Dr. Hicks he made a tour of England in search of Anglo-Saxon MSS., of which he prepared a catalogue.

John Tipper the original publisher of the Ladies' Diary, which commenced in 1704, was also a native of Coventry, and master of the Bablake school.

CITY ARMS. The City Arms are—party per pale, *gules* and *vert;* an elephant *argent,* on a mount *proper,* bearing a castle tripletowered on his back, *or.* Crest—a Cat of Mountain. The cognizance of the Prince of Wales has also been used by the City ever since its assumption by Edward, the Black Prince. CITY OR CORPORATION REVENUE. The annual revenue of the Corporation of Coventry derived from estates, according to the last published accounts, is £1913; from market tolls and stallage £362; and from cattle-marking fees £69. The street and watch rates amount to about £2850 a year.

Lightning Source UK Ltd.
Milton Keynes UK
UKOW021817081112

201914UK00007B/36/P

9 781236 188953